RAND ARROYO CENTER

Identifying Promising Approaches to U.S. Army Institutional Change

A Review of the Literature on Organizational Culture and Climate

Lisa S. Meredith, Carra S. Sims, Benjamin Saul Batorsky,
Adeyemi Okunogbe, Brittany L. Bannon, Craig A. Myatt

Prepared for the United States Army
Approved for public release; distribution unlimited

For more information on this publication, visit www.rand.org/t/RR1588

Library of Congress Cataloging-in-Publication Data is available for this publication.
ISBN: 978-0-8330-9602-9

Published by the RAND Corporation, Santa Monica, Calif.

Cover image courtesy of Shutterstock.com.

Preface

This report documents research conducted for a project entitled "Identifying Promising Approaches to U.S. Army Institutional Change: A Review of the Literature on Organizational Culture and Climate." The project's purpose was to review the literature on organizational culture and climate to identify promising approaches to help address some of the Army's greatest challenges, including behavioral health treatment stigma, negative workplace behaviors, and the growing participation of women in combat-forward roles.

This report distills the results of the literature review, identifying key drivers of cultural change. It also describes how a group of subject-matter experts analyzed the results of that review by identifying the most important drivers of cultural change for the Army. Its findings should interest researchers and policy makers in the Army, the military as a whole, and other organizations in general as they must adapt in response to ongoing social changes. In particular, study findings will help guide policy decisions about institutionalizing organizational change in Army culture to cope with the aforementioned issues.

This research was sponsored by the Foundational Science Research Unit of the U.S. Army Research Institute for the Behavioral and Social Sciences and conducted within RAND Arroyo Center's Personnel, Training, and Health Program. RAND Arroyo Center, part of the RAND Corporation, is a federally funded research and development center sponsored by the United States Army.

The Project Unique Identification Code (PUIC) for the project that produced this document is HQD156920.

Contents

Figures and Tables

Figures

Tables

Summary

Background, Purpose, and Approach

The U.S. Army is confronting a number of challenges. It has relatively well-established organizations and procedures for some challenges, such as force strength reductions. Other challenges are more difficult. These include combat stress and family issues that crop up as a result of repeated deployments. Some soldiers' perceptions that seeking help for stress is a sign of weakness complicate these challenges. Other difficult issues pertain to the workplace, including sexual harassment and assault.

Qualitative research has characterized the current Army's culture as high-stress and "hypermasculine" in that it has strong norms that discourage disclosures or seeking help for emotional concerns, coupled with norms for unhealthy behaviors, such as substance use and violence among personnel. Long-term solutions to such challenges very likely require changes in Army organizational culture and climate. Because many of these challenges are intertwined (e.g., sexual harassment incidents might also involve substance use or abuse), a comprehensive approach is necessary. Change at the institutional level in large organizations, however, is typically very difficult.

In recognition of this difficulty, the U.S. Army Research Institute for the Behavioral and Social Sciences (ARI) asked the RAND Arroyo Center to review the literature on organizational culture and climate to identify promising approaches that the Army might adopt in confronting some of these challenges, especially in the areas of behavioral health stigma and negative workplace behaviors. RAND Arroyo Center researchers identified literature in relevant fields, such as psychology, behavioral sciences, organizational behavior, and anthropology, that pertained to groups such as the military, first responders, and sports organizations; analyzed that literature to identify approaches that could drive culture change; and then vetted those approaches with subject-matter experts (SMEs) in military organizations and processes.

Findings

In reviewing the literature, RAND Arroyo Center researchers and SMEs identified the top five drivers of cultural change. These drivers are listed in Table S.1.

The drivers judged most critical to cultural change in the Army are **goals** and **accountability**. The former is typical of Army processes, in which the leader sets goals by stating intent and personnel at subordinate levels work to realize that intent. Accountability is seen as an inherent part of leadership in that responsibility is fixed at every leadership level. **Training** is a continuous process in and of itself, but it is not sufficient to change culture and climate. It must operate in concert with the other drivers. For example, bottom-up or "grass-roots" approaches, such as a front-line supervisor who emulates a particular climate of respect within his or her unit, would necessarily work in concert with top-down processes, such as formal training or selection by leaders higher in the chain of command. Any institutional change requires **resources**, and time is a critical resource, particularly for leadership. Leaders have many things to attend to, and time devoted to one activity means less time for another. Finally, formal and informal leaders must also be **engaged**. The Army has leaders at every level, from the squad leader to the chief of staff. But some leaders are informal. Communication across all levels of leadership will maximize alignment and effective change implementation.

Additionally, panel discussions identified the following four actions as a first step in affecting culture and climate change.

1. **Define the problem**.
2. **Understand current culture** in relation to a problem but at a general enough level to enable a holistic course of action.
3. **Define/articulate the desired culture or vision.** Note that "vision" is the level at which senior leaders would engage with the problem. Such a definition would be similar to the Australian Army's "Statement of Cultural Intent," which was articulated before an extensive years-long culture change effort and is now a priority second only to supporting personnel and operations. Another way to

Table S.1
Key Drivers and Descriptions for Army Change

Driver	Description
Goals	Setting goals, coherent planning, persistence, and strategic, inspirational, innovative thinking; results oriented
Accountability	Underscoring shared responsibilities and accountability
Training	Developing personnel through training (skills, engagement, education)
Resources	Devoting sufficient resources (finances, staff, time) to change
Engagement	Engaging both formal and informal leaders (stakeholders)

define the desired vision would be seeking what a panelist called a "Culture of Trust."

4. **Identify specific goals.** Note that "goals" is the level at which operational/tactical implementation–level leaders would engage with the problem.

These steps are consistent with what is found in the literature.

Additionally, panel members made the following points about implementing culture change. First, a holistic approach that focuses drivers in a coordinated way is necessary to effect change that persists. This approach differs from a "crisis-response" approach that treats a persistent cultural problem as a transient issue; once the immediate crisis passes, the problem is likely to reappear because no true institutional change has occurred. Second, the panel emphasized the need for clarity and specificity in articulating both problems and desired solutions. Third, it is necessary to engage people at different levels of the organization. While the Army is a hierarchical organization in which direction flows from the top, it is also an organization in which leadership responsibility exists at virtually every level. Therefore, low-level leaders need to be engaged in the change process to ensure it occurs at all levels.

Conclusions

Definitions of Organizational Culture

The literature identifies more than 80 definitions of organizational culture that could apply to the Army. A suitable definition of culture for the Army should accommodate depth, openness, and both top-down and bottom-up change. This definition is a good starting point:

> Culture is a pattern of shared basic assumptions, invented, discovered, or developed by a given group as it learns to cope with its problems of external adaptation and internal integration that has worked well enough to be considered valid, and, therefore, is to be taught to new members of the group as the correct way to perceive, think, and feel in relation to those problems reframing. (Schein, 1990)

Drivers of Culture and Climate Change

Of the many drivers of change we reviewed, several align particularly well with the existing Army culture and are feasible within the military structure. The top five drivers relevant to the Army are listed in Table S.1.

Applying Approaches

Organizational culture change is difficult, made more so by the fact that the theory of change outstrips the practice, and clear evidence of successful organizational culture change is sparse. The fact that such aggregate-level change also requires changing the values, beliefs, attitudes, and behaviors of many individuals further complicates organization change. However, changing individual attitudes is difficult, and it is not clear whether those changes must precede institutional change or whether broader changes at the institutional level facilitate sufficient change in an individual's life to precipitate shifts in important attitudes (Lewin, 1947). But organizational culture change can work, and the drivers uncovered in the literature reviews and interactions with SMEs provide a good starting point.

Recommendations

We offer eight recommendations for developers of doctrine and policy interested in driving organizational culture change to address the Army's biggest challenges. Our recommendations are framed broadly, and Army leaders would need to adjust these recommendations to a specific context in any attempts to implement change.

Define Organizational Culture

We recommend that, initially at least, the Army adopts the Schein definition of culture. The Army may wish to modify that definition as it gains experience in changing its culture.

Adopt a Common Definition of Army Organizational Culture

We suggest that the Army adopt a new definition of organizational culture that is both specific enough to fit with the Army domain and general enough to cover changes that occur within that domain. It should guide the Army to accomplish the following:

- Address multiple levels to manifest desired culture change through values and ideologies as well as symbols and artifacts
- Align policies with the practices, competencies, and perceptions of organizational members
- Use both a top-down and bottom-up approach, involving strategic and formalized processes as well as informal socialization processes
- Convey an openness to change to set the tone for continually adapting to change and transformation.

We recommend this because it is important to work from a common framework when attempting institutional culture change.

Determine Target Problems Amenable to Culture Change

We recommend that the Army avoid attempting to change the entire organizational culture, but rather undertake specific, problem-focused organizational culture change. Given that organizational culture change is often a time- and other resource–consuming endeavor, the change effort should be sufficiently focused. Also, outsiders to the organization may be able to identify some of the less visible aspects of culture (e.g., basic assumptions that guide policies, practices, and organizational behavior) in conjunction with insiders.

Assess the Culture and Climate in the Problem Context

We also recommend that the Army assess the current culture and climate to enable dealing with the most pressing problems. The Army is a large organization with diverse missions, skill sets, and suborganizations. It may be impossible to encompass its culture or climate except in generalities. The emphasis should be placed on those elements of culture that are relevant to a problem, not the entire culture. However, a holistic approach can be applied when using a specific problem set as a springboard and when setting parameters. Culture change should also involve various aspects of human resource management, such as training, incentives, and work design, as well as information and controlling systems.

Prioritize Organizational Culture Change

We recommend that senior Army leaders clearly articulate strategic goals, prioritizing competing values and initiatives (e.g., core values emphasizing personal sacrifice and obeying orders might be implicitly at odds with resilience initiatives) or delegate that authority appropriately; instill trust at all organizational levels that appropriate actions will be supported; and allocate sufficient time, training, measurement, tracking capacity, and finances to maximize cultural change.

Develop a Strategy for Change with Clear Goals

We recommend that the Army develop a clear strategy and goals to guide change planning and implementation. A change effort organized around clear goals, coupled with other individual behavior change efforts, is more likely to be institutionalized. Emphasizing personal accountability and responsibility for expected behavior may make it possible for change to happen even before formal policy implementation, which can often take a long time to formulate and implement.

Engage Stakeholders at All Levels

We recommend that the Army engage all levels of leadership through the command chain to address both overarching goals and those specific to different subcultures. Typically in the Army, directions for change issue from the top and flow down to subordinate levels. That, of course, must occur, but leadership must also pay attention to local issues, particularly to address the more specific goals of the different subcultures in such a large and diverse force. This may include engaging individuals who are outside of established chains of command, but whose local influence is strong, such as chaplains.

Consider Targeted Training to Maximize Resources and Uptake

To maximize uptake of new skills, we recommend that trainees have opportunities to practice new skills and incorporate them into processes. We also recommend targeting training strategically to subgroups (e.g., certain units or subcultures) to maximize success. In addition to targeting both formal and informal leaders to influence their institutional unit members, it may be important to target some types of training to leaders to prioritize focus areas. Capabilities-based assessments can be structured to determine training requirements, especially when Army doctrine and education do not fully address emerging or changing policy. An organization can use capabilities-based assessments to recategorize mission-enhancing training as mission-essential or mission-critical training (e.g., classes on drinking and driving, sexual harassment training).

Acknowledgments

The authors thank the members of the subject-matter expert panel who helped us interpret the literature review findings. Panelists included members of the U.S. Army and Air Force, RAND researchers, and a member of a partner nation army. We also thank the panel observers from ARI, Dr. Melinda Key-Roberts and Kaitlin Thomas, for their insights during the panel discussion. Additionally, we thank LTC Heather Smigowski (who was serving at the time as a RAND Army Research fellow) for reviewing and validating portions of the report and both Rosie Velasquez and Jamie Greenberg for their help with project meeting logistics and report preparation. We are grateful for the guidance from our project officers at ARI, Dr. Miliani Jimenez, Dr. Jessica Gallus, and Dr. Gerald (Jay) Goodwin. Finally, we would like to thank peer reviewers Dr. Mark Ehrhart, from San Diego State University, and Dr. Kirsten Keller, from the RAND Corporation.

Abbreviations

AR	Army Regulation
ARI	U.S. Army Research Institute for the Behavioral and Social Sciences
PTSD	posttraumatic stress disorder
SME	subject-matter expert

CHAPTER ONE

Introduction

Background and Context

The variety of issues faced by 21st century U.S. Army leadership charged with shaping organizational culture and climate affect military and civilian personnel across all ranks and at all levels. The Army is leading a campaign to optimize human performance by creating a conceptual strategic framework that requires individual adaptability and institutional agility. That framework expands the Army's capability to develop a culture that values the human aspects of exploiting a decisive cognitive edge, physical supremacy, and cultural understanding over potential adversaries (United States Army Combined Arms Center, 2014).

The Army anticipates that its future force will need to innovate rapidly in environments often filled with volatility, uncertainty, complexity, and ambiguity. Therefore, there is an increasing demand to build an institutional culture and climate capable of addressing a diverse set of challenges. As contemporary examples, the Army is increasingly aware of and attending to challenges posed by negative workplace behaviors (e.g., sexual assault, hazing, toxic leadership); changing demographics, including the lifting of longstanding gender restrictions, such as the ban on women in combat units (see Farris and Hepner, 2014; Miller, et al., 2012; Ramchand et al., 2011); and behavioral health challenges (e.g., suicide and suicidal ideation).

The U.S. Army is not alone in its need to innovate. Several armies among partnering nations are doing the same. Australia, for example, is calling upon its army to adapt and innovate, examining conduct and behavior, gender issues, and technological change (Australian Army, 2009). Moreover, as a general principle, both civilian and military organizations face a need to adapt in response to ongoing social and other environmental changes. An examination of change for the Army can potentially benefit from a broader perspective.

It is useful to dissect the challenges facing the Army by exploring them in the context of specific issues of concern. One general area of concern is negative workplace behavior or misconduct (Dalal, 2005; Gruys and Sackett, 2003; Robinson and

Bennett, 1995), which includes specific issues like sexual harassment and assault (Morral, Gore, and Schell, 2014) and substance use, including alcohol abuse (United States Department of Defense, 2013). War's behavioral health consequences pose a second challenge. While the majority of Army servicemembers fare well after deployment, others face a range of behavioral health challenges, including posttraumatic stress disorder (PTSD) and depression (Miller, et al., 2012); suicide and suicidal ideation (e.g., Ramchand et al., 2011); and stress from combat, isolation, and other sources. In addition to the behavioral health challenges themselves, some soldiers are concerned about a perceived stigma associated with seeking help for emotional concerns (Acosta et al., 2014). These concerns arise in the context of a major drawdown and shifting demographics, as personnel adjust to changes in the roles available to women in the Army. Changes to tackle these issues, as well as others that arise, could potentially represent major shifts for the Army—changes that may not align optimally with the current organizational culture and climate. Therefore, some perspective on the literature on culture and climate may offer the Army suggestions on how to manage these and any other challenges it may face going forward.

Why Culture and Climate Are Relevant

For the Army to adapt quickly and responsively to rapid societal change, technological change, and a multitude of newly emerging threat scenarios, it must itself change. "Culture" and "climate" are two approaches often used for organizational change efforts (Martins, 2011) that offer a systemic approach to challenges that often manifest at a more individual level, such as suicide, harassment, and assault. Organizational culture is often seen as tapping into the underlying "why" of organizational behavior (e.g., values, attitudes), while climate is seen more as the "what" of organizations (e.g., policies, rewards, and punishments; see Ostroff, Kinicki, and Muhammad, 2012; Schneider, Ehrhart, and Macey, 2011; and Zohar and Hofmann, 2012, for some recent reviews).[1] While "climate change" deals with employees' perceptions of current practices, policies, and implementation (and is more closely related to the behaviors mentioned above), the underlying culture must be changed as well, as it permeates all organizational activities and behaviors and sets the stage for climates to emerge.

Army leadership highlights the importance of innovation and change in official doctrine, especially in the context of soldier development (Army Regulation [AR] 600-100, 2007). The Army's emphasis on change, though, is distinct from organizational culture change; the former has often emphasized external factors (e.g., political control, competition) and managerial efforts to aid performance within some domain (e.g., innovation; Fernandez and Rainey, 2006) as opposed to organizational culture

[1] We discuss similarities and differences in greater depth later.

change's focus on human processes (e.g., informal socialization of values, behavioral norms). Despite a lack of consensus about the process of organizational change, evidence from a wide range of empirical studies with an emphasis on public organizations suggests that leaders can in fact effect large-scale strategic change by ensuring a need for change; developing clear goals and a detailed plan; building support and overcoming resistance; creating champions for change; attracting outside support; applying sufficient resources; integrating the change into formal doctrine or policy; and using a holistic approach (Fernandez and Rainey, 2006).[2] In the broader organizational change literature, culture is simply cited as a bottom-up factor (one of many, including organization size) that might predict the success of a given organizational change effort (e.g., a risk-taking culture and innovation success; Fernandez and Rainey, 2006). Thus, it can be both a target and determinant of change within an organization (Burke, 2014). Moreover, it should be noted that prescriptions specific to climate or culture change bear strong resemblance to the more general organizational change tactics (e.g., recommendations for developing clear goals and plans, which may include relevant metrics, and integrating change into policies or procedures, which echo Schein's 2004 leader-driven culture embedding techniques and Schneider, Ehrhart, and Macey's 2011 recommendations for shaping a climate). Given the Army's need to adapt continuously to external demands and recent strategic plans to promote force resilience, culture is an important target for setting up the adaptive development of the organization in a broader sense. However, the literature on culture and climate itself is very wide ranging and diffuse and not easily digestible to leaders. These circumstances combine to warrant a new review of culture and climate and how best to apply these constructs to meet the needs of the Army.

Research Goals and Objective

The Army asked the RAND Arroyo Center to provide a comprehensive review of the literature on organizational culture and climate to identify promising approaches that the Army might adopt in confronting some of the current challenges, such as behavioral health stigma and increasing negative workplace behaviors. While much of our report describes our research process and findings, we also present general recommendations that will require specification to each change effort. We examined literature pertaining to both organizational culture and climate, because both provide valu-

[2] There are many theories or perspectives of how organizational change occurs. Some, for example, emphasize a linear transformation wherein all institutions go through a set of predefined phases as a function of naturally occurring disruptions and competition (e.g., life cycle perspective, Burke, 2014; Fernandez and Rainey, 2006) or external selection processes that determine an organization's ultimate survival (e.g., evolutionary theory; Burke, 2014; Fernandez and Rainey, 2006); others suggest a more planned approach with management in the driver's seat (e.g., rational adaptive theories and policy diffusion models, Fernandez and Rainey, 2006).

able perspective in managing organizational change, and moreover as noted by Day, Griffin, and Louw (2014) they are sometimes used interchangeably or the term "culture" is used in the general sense. Following this convention we occasionally do this but more generally use the specific terms.

Given the broad purview of our task, we focused on answering the following research questions.

1. How is organizational culture defined?
2. What drives/maintains particular cultures or subcultures?
3. How can we apply promising approaches to institutional change from a variety of industries to the Army?

Organization of This Report

The remainder of this report consists of three chapters and five appendixes. In Chapter Two, we present the study approach to the literature review along with how we vetted preliminary review findings with a subject-matter expert (SME) panel. In Chapter Three, we present the results from the review and identify key drivers of institutional change and strategies for promoting cultural change in the Army. Finally, in Chapter Four we present conclusions and make initial recommendations for identifying promising approaches to institutional change. The appendixes provide more detail about the literature review abstraction tool, a bibliography of the literature included in the review along with links to the document sources, definitions of organizational culture abstracted from the literature, the SME panelist rating form, and the summary table of the panel discussion itself with feedback from the panelists incorporated.

CHAPTER TWO

Study Approach

In this chapter, we discuss the research questions, including how culture and climate are defined and distinguished in the literature as well as in the Army. We then move on to how we addressed each question. We begin with the literature review and then explain how we benefited from the input of six experts using a group panel format. We culminate this chapter by describing some strengths and caveats of this research process.

Research Tasks

To address the project objective and research questions, we took the following steps:

- Reviewed the literature on organizational culture and climate, and change
- Coded, analyzed, and synthesized the results from the literature review to identify definitions, subcultures, and drivers of organizational change
- Convened a discussion group with SMEs to:
  - Rate the literature-derived drivers prior to the SME discussion
  - Prioritize the rated drivers in terms of alignment with Army mission and feasibility for implementing change based on feedback from the discussion
- Identified promising approaches for realigning Army culture to embrace policy changes.

Defining Culture and Climate

Our first undertaking was to define culture and climate and examine their similarities and differences. The Army defines both culture and climate in AR 600-100 and other published regulations; however, those definitions are general and lack the scientific depth for evidence-based studies or staff analysis for capabilities-based assessments. The Army definition of culture is as follows:

> The set of long-held values, beliefs, expectations, and practices shared by a group that signifies what is important and influences how an organization operates. (AR 600-100, 2007, p. 21)

The Army also defines climate as "The state of morale and level of satisfaction of members of an organization" (AR 600-100, 2007).

As noted earlier in this document,

> Army culture is a consequence of customs, traditions, ideals, ethos, values, and norms of conduct that have existed for more than 230 years. The moral and ethical tenets of the U.S. Constitution, the Declaration of Independence, and the Army Values [Loyalty, Duty, Respect, Selfless Service, Honor, Integrity, and Personal Courage] characterize the Army's professionalism and culture, and describe the ethical standards expected of all Army leaders. (AR 600-100, 2007, p. 1)

This statement aligns with Soeters's observation that in pursuing organizational culture change, organizations such as the military must balance tradition with the needs of the present (Soeters, 2000). Moreover, while these definitions have value to the Army and speak to the centuries of history and tradition, for purposes of change implementation, it may be helpful to craft definitions to the specific purpose of culture or climate change that employ more particulars as described below.

Both culture and climate are organization-level constructs composed of aggregated individual employee-level constructs (Denison, 1996). At the organizational level, culture includes *shared* employee attitudes, beliefs, values, norms, and symbols and is often seen as tapping into the underlying "why" of organizational behavior. Meanwhile, organizational climate typically focuses more on employees' *shared* perceptions of the "what" of organizational policies and practices, such as rewards and punishments (although there are variations on these themes; see Ostroff, Kinicki, and Muhammad, 2012; Schneider, Ehrhart, and Macey, 2011; and Zohar and Hofmann, 2012, for some recent reviews). Leaders play a critical role in establishing and maintaining both culture and climate through similar behaviors (Ehrhart, Schneider, and Macey, 2014).

For both culture and climate, issues of strength and alignment are relevant. In the work on climate, this is typically considered through measures of consensus or agreement among employees on a given issue (see Ostroff, Kinicki, and Muhammad, 2012). Ostroff, Kinicki, and Muhammad discuss the creation of climate strength in terms of creating a strong situation (see also Bowen and Ostroff, 2004). A "strong situation" is one that minimizes the effects of individual preferences and personalities on behavior and promotes conformity. To extend this to organizational life, consistent policies, procedures, and practices create little ambiguity in messaging and a shared climate among employees subject to the messaging—that is, a strong climate produces consistent interpretation and behavior. In contrast, culture strength is sometimes discussed, but not in as consistent a manner (Ostroff, Kinicki, and Muhammad, 2012) and discussions of fragmentation and subcultures are more common in the culture domain (Schneider, Ehrhart, and Macey, 2011). Ehrhart, Schneider, and Macey (2014) do discuss culture strength in terms of alignment. Although alignment may be considered from multiple perspectives, the authors offer that internal alignment of the various aspects of culture and the resultant structures, processes, and communications is likely to create a strong culture. As with climate, a strong culture promotes agreement on common perceptions (although about values, symbols, etc.) and more consistency in behavior.

Climate is quite often currently conceptualized as being climate *for* some strategic goal, such as innovation or safety, although there have been attempts to create theoretically based global climate measures (Schneider, Ehrhart, and Macey, 2011; Zohar and Hofmann, 2012). Culture is more likely to be approached as a global characteristic of the organization, although popular operationalizations posit some general dimensions (Ostroff, Kinicki, and Muhammad, 2012; Schneider, Ehrhart, and Macey, 2011; Zohar and Hofmann, 2012). Thus, culture and climate are closely related but not the same constructs, although the literature is somewhat confused on this distinction and often uses the terms interchangeably (Day, Griffin, and Louw, 2014). As suggested by Ostroff, Kinicki, and Muhammad (2012), the root of conflation may rest in the empirical rather than theoretical literature.

However, both culture and climate change are necessary to effect comprehensive culture change; as a result, the literature included in this review encompasses both. Whereas culture is viewed as a more stable, historically rooted process that includes the deep assumptions and values (and the informal socialization of these values) that guide institutional priorities over longer periods, climate provides a snapshot of employees' shared perceptions of current practices and policies (e.g., perceived inconsistencies between espoused beliefs and implicit priorities as dictated by culture). Current attempts to integrate the literatures suggest that climate offers perspective on the underlying values and assumptions of culture and that these values and assumptions affect policies, procedures, and practices that establish climates (Ostroff, Kinicki, and Muhammad, 2012; Schneider, Ehrhart, and Macey, 2011; Zohar and Hofmann, 2012). Thus, current writing specifies that there is interplay between the culture under the surface and the more visible climate manifestations. In other words, climate manifests the "work unit observables" (Burke, 2014) of the underlying culture (Denison, 1996).

We note that there may be many different manifestations of the same underlying culture, which highlights an important consideration for this work: Although organizational climate is theorized to be more amenable to change than organizational culture (though still difficult, given its many components; Burke, 2014), focusing exclusively on changing practices or employees' attitudes and behaviors without also addressing problematic assumptions or values might only result in a different manifestation of the same underlying cultural problem. Conversely, focusing exclusively on creating a new vision for culture change and transforming institutional values does not ensure that behavioral movement toward that change will occur (Burke, 2014). As Ostroff, Kinicki, and Tamkins (2003; see also Ostroff, Kinicki, and Muhammad, 2012; Zohar and Hofmann, 2014) have suggested, the ultimate goal of work in this area might be to promote adaptive consistency between organizational culture and climate through appropriate practices (e.g., how rule violators are dealt with; how mental health challenges are reported and treated in actuality). In any event, as noted by Schneider, Ehrhart, and Maccy (2011), many of the cultural embedding mechanisms proposed by Schein serve quite well as pointers on how to change climate, as well. Burke (2014) even proposes focusing on behavior over attitudes in terms of change targets, noting that behaviors can precede and affect attitudes.

As may be clear from the discussion of alignment and consistency, a holistic approach to change is generally recommended—that is, specific change initiatives should work in concert rather than competing with one another. Despite the necessity of holism, understanding the whole of any organizational culture (and subcultures and climates) is not necessarily feasible. Hence, a holistic perspective should be applied to the aspects of climate and culture pertinent to the specific change effort.

Characterizing the Army's Current Culture

The Army's culture has been characterized as a high-stress, "hyper-masculine" culture (Bucher, 2011) that emphasizes core values of integrity through self-sacrifice, teamwork, and obedience and includes strong norms against emotional disclosure or seeking help for behavioral health. Although there is a strong, collective "Army" identity within the organization, qualitative research has revealed less emphasis on its individual members and a perceived lack of autonomy among enlisted personnel (Bucher, 2011). The Army also historically has had the most occupational restrictions placed on women and one of the lowest percentages of female personnel (Miller et al., 2012). As the Army faces shifting gender demographics, with more women entering previously restricted combat roles, it may have to adapt to maintain unit cohesion. To address strong masculine norms and integrate the changing roles of women, a more holistic approach is necessary, encompassing both climate and culture change.

The Army is certainly not alone in its challenges, and it has cultural overlaps with several other high-stress, traditionally masculine-oriented industries covered in this review. These settings include first-response and paramilitary organizations, medicine, higher education, for-profit corporate settings, and professional and college-level team sports. Cultural overlaps hierarchical structures and elements of bureaucracy; demands for time and energy from members (e.g., military personnel as well as their families); and challenges with member behavioral and mental health (e.g., sexual harassment, toxic leadership, hazing new members).

Importantly, subcultures (subgroups of an organization with their own values, beliefs, and behavior) are also commonly observed within these organizations. For example, two subcultures often exist within uniformed organizations, such as first responders and the military (Soeters, 2000). These are the "cold" organization, or the subgroup charged with preparing for action (civilian employees, high-level staff), and the "hot" organization, or those involved in carrying out the actions of the organization (active personnel in infantry divisions). Targeted change efforts must acknowledge the presence of subcultures, because they can serve as sources of resistance or champions of organizational culture or climate change.

The definitions of organizational culture and climate speak to why and how these concepts are relevant to organizational change efforts. The context of the Army speaks to specific issues and complexities that should be kept in mind when considering such an undertaking. Given this grounding, we turn to the specific methodology we used to review and synthesize the literature.

Study Methods

Literature Review

Our specific objective was to review the literature on organizational culture and climate to identify documents most relevant to understanding promising approaches to organizational change in the Army. The review involved five stages: (1) selecting relevant data sources, (2) developing a search strategy for the sources selected, (3) constructing an abstraction tool, (4) screening the results of the search, and (5) coding and analyzing the findings. In the following sections, we describe each of these stages in sequence.

Data Source Selection

We selected six industries to include in our review: the military, first responders, health and medicine, professional sports, private sector corporations, and education. We also had a general category. Our review focused on organizational culture and climate change in high-stress, traditionally masculine-oriented settings (cultures of "toughness") because they might lend themselves more naturally to the military culture. These settings included paramilitary and first responder organizations (e.g., police, fire, emergency medicine), which bear the greatest similarities to military culture in that they are "uniformed organizations" that demand a lot of time and energy from their members (Soeters, 2000). We also drew upon literature that describes how best to manage large-scale changes in the military, such as "Don't Ask, Don't Tell" (National Defense Research Institute, 2010), as well as Army guidance and other materials intending to promote change within the Army, such as the Army's Ready and Resilient Campaign (United States Army Medical Department, undated). We included sports because teams work as units, and historically a culture of "toughness" has prevailed in that domain as well. Finally, other areas have a robust literature on culture and/or climate change (health/medicine and private sector corporate) that we thought would provide perspective on change in the military. We identified and coded the literature from these industries to consider potential industry-specific moderating factors and how those might affect our findings.

Search Strategy

Our primary search focused on identifying peer-reviewed citations from six databases:

- PsycINFO
- Business Source Complete
- Academic Search Complete
- MEDLINE
- Defense policy literature (Defense Technical Information Center)
- RAND publications (RAND Online Catalog System).

We used the following search terms:

- organization
- culture OR climate
- change
- transform
- adapt
- modify
- innovate
- intervention
- learn
- behavior
- NOT "climate change."

We set our time frame from January 1, 2001, through July 31, 2014. This start date enabled us to cover nearly 15 years of literature. In addition, 9/11 was likely a significant trigger of culture change for the Army. As noted by others (Wong, Bliese, and McGurk, 2003), President George W. Bush saw 9/11 as an indication that leadership and the culture of leadership needed to change to meet the new challenges faced by national security. Including that seminal event capitalizes on the possibility that culture change was more extensive and/or more rapid at that point and generated reporting on culture and/or climate change efforts. Given that we also included recent literature reviews of general climate and culture as well as change in that context (Burke, 2011; Schneider, Ehrhart, and Macey, 2011; Zohar and Hofmann, 2012), we achieved reasonable coverage overall. We do not cover the larger literature on organizational change and development, as that would have been beyond the scope of our present study. We summarize our specific inclusion and exclusion criteria in the following list.

We *included* all documents that:

- explicitly discuss organizational culture or climate, subcultures, or the process of organizational transformation as a primary focus
- pertain to one of the following industries: military, education, first-response, health/medicine, corporate, and sports.

We *excluded* documents from review that:

- were published before January 2001
- were not peer-reviewed, published works (e.g., theses)
- were not in English or included a non-U.S. sample
- had only a secondary focus on organizational culture/climate
- did not include one of the listed industries
- were not cleared for open publication.

Literature Abstraction

We developed a tool for systematically abstracting information from the 549 documents we identified as relevant. We intentionally focused on the following seven key elements to characterize each of the documents.

1. document type (whether empirical—experiment or observational versus theoretical, review, or policy report)
2. data collection method (quantitative, qualitative, mixed methods)
3. industry (military, first response, health/medical, professional sports, corporate, education, or general/other)
4. subcultures (orthogonal, enhancing, and countercultures)
5. culture change mechanism (selection, training/development, monitoring/control)
6. content (values/attitudes/beliefs, norms, symbols, or knowledge/skills/resources)
7. outcomes (financial, behavioral, social, psychological, or other).

We chose these elements because we wanted to learn whether there would be differences in the type of content (i.e., culture, climate, subculture) for documents published in different forms (type of presentation, study design) and industries. We also wanted to examine whether there would be different patterns of covering the culture and climate content across type of document and industry.

We classified subcultures into the three types consistent with Martin and Siehl (1983). They describe an enhancing subculture as one that either enhances or augments preestablished organizational norms and values. An orthogonal subculture is similar to an enhancing subculture in that it, too, adheres to the core values of the larger organizational culture. However, orthogonal subcultures also uphold values that are distinct from those of the dominant culture. Note that these values do not conflict with the core values reflective of the larger organizational culture. A counterculture is a subculture that upholds values that directly conflict with those characterizing the dominant organizational culture.

We also abstracted portions of text for any definitions of organizational culture or climate provided and coded both the "drivers" of organizational culture/climate or transformation (including maintaining factors, facilitators, and barriers to change) and policy recommendations or lessons as described in each document.

Before finalizing our abstraction tool, the research team randomly selected a subset of ten documents for each of the five team members to code using our literature abstraction tool. We reviewed and discussed the initial coding as a team. We resolved discrepancies until we all agreed on the approach and established intercoder agreement. More details about the literature review abstraction tool, including the full set of coding options and operational definitions, are provided in Appendix A.

Document Screening

Figure 2.1 shows the flow of our document review process. We identified nearly 4,000 documents from our initial search and randomly assigned them to three coders. At the first stage, based on title and abstract screening, we excluded 40 percent of the documents because they did not meet our criteria for inclusion (they came from international sources or were irrelevant because neither culture nor climate was the focus). We excluded another 549 documents because they covered international content not

Figure 2.1
Flow of Two-Stage Screening Process for Identifying Documents

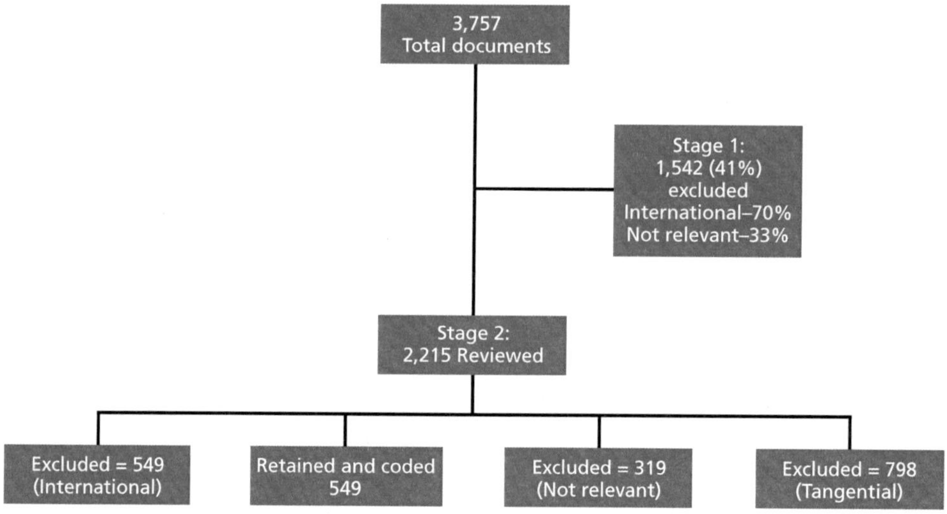

RAND *RR1588-2.1*

deemed relevant to our topic,[1] 319 because they were not relevant for some other reason, and 798 because they dealt with topics only tangential to our focus (including other industries). For example, an irrelevant article did not mention culture/climate or mentioned culture/climate in a context outside of organizations (e.g., surveys of differences in perspective by religious culture). An article with a topic tangential to our focus may have mentioned culture, but not used it in analysis or used it in analysis but not provided results or recommendations relevant to organizational culture. We validated our screening strategy by having two independent coders screen a randomly selected subset of 200 documents (100 per coder) and compared these results with the initial screening results (yielding a 75 percent consistency rate). We then discussed any discrepancies as a group to reach consensus before moving on to the second-stage review. After exclusions, we retained 549 documents to code. A complete bibliography of these documents is provided in Appendix B.

Coding and Data Analysis

Three elements from the literature review required additional coding of free text that was abstracted into the review tool. These elements included definitions of culture or climate along with drivers of organizational change and policy recommendations. We further coded definitions of organizational culture[2] along four dimensions:

1. **Level**, surface level (structures, symbols, stories, policies, etc.) and "the way things are done" (Schein, 2000; cited in Schneider et al., 2011), compared with deep level (assumptions, values/attitudes/beliefs, etc.) and more about "why things are done"
2. **Specificity**, either general or domain-specific ("Army culture" is general, but "culture of respect" or "culture of safety" is domain-specific)
3. **Development**, whether the definitions are "top-down," with strategic socialization by leaders, or "bottom-up," in which development arises from members' shared values, perceptions, or daily interactions
4. **Receptivity**, whether openness to change (culture is a changing or transformative construct) or resistance to change (culture as a stable or rigid construct).

---

[1] As noted by Martins (2011), the body of change literature that takes into account national culture has grown in recent years and allows for analysis of this contextual element. National culture is certainly expected to be relevant to organizational culture (e.g., Hofstede and Hofstede, 2005; Schein, 2004). We determined that it would potentially be a conflating factor for our purposes and hence excluded articles that crossed national and organizational culture/climate.

[2] We also coded only general definitions, not domain-specific ones, because we wanted to maximize the potential for transportability to the Army. We chose to restrict our more detailed coding of definitions only for those that defined organizational culture, as that was the specific task and most definitions of climate were similar to those of culture but with more context specificity. However, note that the dimension of level does include some aspect of what is generally considered to be climate in the surface pole (i.e., "what things are done"; Ostroff, Kinicki, and Muhammad, 2012).

To ensure accuracy of coding, we double coded a subset of the first 30 definitions, discussed any inconsistencies, and recoded until reaching agreement. Table 2.1 provides examples for each type of definition.

Using the information abstracted on drivers and policy recommendations, two members of the research team coded the content into different categories of drivers. Many of the documents covered content in more than a single category, so these are not intended to be mutually exclusive. We used a combination of bottom-up coding

Table 2.1
Example Definitions for Coding Elements

Dimensions	Descriptions[a]	Examples
Level	Deep	The values, attitudes, beliefs, orientations, and underlying assumptions prevalent among people in a society (Harrison and Huntington, 2000, as cited in Linnean, 2007[b])
	Surface	Organizational practices and the consequences of those practices (Clayton et al., 1997, as cited in Bumstead and Boyce, 2004[a])
	Deep and surface	The transmitted patterns of values, beliefs and expectations shared by people, including the system of symbols which imparts them to members of the group (Schreyögg et al., 1995, as cited in Voelpel, Leibold, and Streb, 2005[a])
Specificity	General	The culture of an organization consists of its norms, values, and beliefs, and is reflected by its stories, rituals and rites, symbols, and language (Daft, 2000, as cited in Zazzali et al., 2007[a])
	Domain-specific	Definition of the patient safety culture of an organization is "the product of individual and group values, attitudes, perceptions, competencies, and patterns of behavior that determine the commitment to, and the style and proficiency of, an organization's health and safety management" (Great Britain Health and Safety Commission, 1993)
Development	Top-down	An organization's value system, its collection of guiding principles driven by leadership (Evans and Lindsay, 2008, as cited in Wright, 2013[a])
	Bottom-up	No clear example[c]
	Top-down and bottom-up	A system of shared values and beliefs constructed by an organization and by its employees through tangible and intangible cues (Franklin and Pagan, as cited in Nica, 2013)
Receptivity	Open to change	The interaction between environmental variables, organizational practices, and the consequences of those practices (Bumstead and Boyce, 2004)
	Resistant to change	The deep structure of organizations, which is rooted in the values, beliefs, and assumptions held by organizational members and that is "rooted in history, collectively held, and sufficiently complex to resist many attempts at direct manipulation" (Denison, 1996)

[a] We included an "unclear" category in each dimension in which the definitions make no explicit or implicit references to any particular description.
[b] See Appendix B for full citation.
[c] We believe this process of development occurs and include it in the table, although we could not find clear examples from our list of definitions of culture.

(examining key words and phrases that were repeatedly mentioned across sources) and a top-down schema informed by knowledge of the culture/climate and implementation literature to develop our coding categories. The two coders initially reviewed the same content and developed independent coding schemas, which were then discussed. Through an iterative process, both stable driver codes and their definitions were developed, and subsequently applied to the abstracted literature review material. The two coders took the stable set of developed codes and independently coded the abstracted material, resolving any discrepancies through discussion.

SME Panel

We used an SME panel to vet the findings from the literature review and to prioritize the drivers of organizational culture change in terms of alignment with Army mission and feasibility of implementation. The purpose of this discussion was to use a participatory approach, involving multiple stakeholders, to review our literature review findings and identify the most promising approach to realign culture and climate in the Army. With that in mind, we solicited panelists with expertise with the literature and an academic perspective as well as panelists with military expertise. We identified not only SMEs with an Army perspective, but also SMEs with perspectives from other services and other nations' military forces. We developed a list of SMEs in collaboration with our action officers and ultimately sent invitations to 22 individuals. Six SMEs ultimately accepted and participated, representing experience in the Army, other U.S. services, and other and national militaries as well as experience in applying research and policy analysis to varied military contexts. As part of the recruitment process and pre-meeting correspondence, we explained the nature of the study and our vision of the SMEs' roles.

We generated a list of drivers in the coding of the literature abstraction form; before coming together for discussion, we asked the panelists to rate the drivers on separate five-point rating scales (see Appendix D) in which higher scores indicated greater alignment to the Army mission and implementation feasibility. We provided space for them to discuss their rating rationale for each driver as well as space to add drivers that they felt should be included. We integrated this feedback into discussion at the panel session.

We began the panel discussion with introductions and a review of the purpose, process, and findings of the literature review portion of the study. We then discussed panelists' aggregated ratings, paying attention to areas of agreement and disagreement and covering the majority of drivers on the form at least briefly. We also discussed additional drivers generated in the pre-meeting exercise, ultimately including two of them by consensus. We concluded the session by prioritizing a subset of drivers for the Army to develop and emphasize going forward. Panelists were asked to nominate their "top three" drivers, and discussion focused on more-specific implementation recommendations for developing a comprehensive approach to influence organizational culture change.

During the course of the discussion, it became clear that some consideration of a general framework as well as some caveats were in order. In our findings, we draw on discussion of this framework as well as the specific discussion surrounding the drivers deemed most important. We provided the summary of the discussion to our SMEs after completion of the panel discussion and asked them to provide feedback and correction where needed (see Appendix E).

Study Caveats

This study contributes to our understanding of organizational culture and climate by identifying some of the most promising approaches to achieving change in these constructs. Nevertheless, some caveats apply to our effort. First, we were limited in how much literature we could cover within the available timeline and resources. The literature is far ranging across different disciplines and industries. To make the review manageable, we purposely selected the databases and industries most relevant to the military context. We also bounded our search to 15 years back in time. To ensure that we did not miss seminal literature from the more distant past, we supplemented the search by including chapters and seminal articles on the topic if they were highly relevant. For example, we include Schein's (1990) *American Psychologist* review article; Denison's 1996 review of similarities and differences between culture and climate; Schneider, Goldstein, and Smith's (1995) update to the Attraction-Selection-Attrition framework; Soeters's (2000) handbook chapter on culture in uniformed organizations; and Burke's 2014 handbook chapter on climate and culture change.

A second caveat about the literature review is that while we sought to achieve consistency across document abstractors and coders, these processes are, by definition, subjective. While we tried to minimize subjectivity by having multiple ratings and discussions among raters to achieve consensus, there may still have been some unavoidable inconsistencies. To code the drivers of organizational change and policy recommendations, we used a pile sort technique to derive categories of similar drivers and held iterative discussions to reach consensus.

Our approach to the literature review was not to summarize all of the documents in the traditional manner. Rather, we sought to target our reviews so that we could focus on salient information. We did this using a standardized abstraction tool to maximize consistency among the reviewers. Moreover, what we provide is not a traditional meta-analysis in which we compile effect sizes. Although feasible for subsets of our article compilation, our scope was so broad and the literature so diverse it precluded this approach.

The panel discussion with experts, while a clear improvement over relying strictly on the literature, also had some limitations. The experiences and views of the small group of six individuals are unlikely to represent the views of all academic and military experts. However, we intentionally included a range of disciplinary perspectives among military research experts (an industrial/organizational psychologist and a sociologist) and active duty servicemembers from the U.S. and Australian Armies, as well as the U.S. Air Force. Thus, the vetting process in collaboration with the sponsor covered several possible perspectives.

CHAPTER THREE

Definitions and Drivers of Organizational Culture and Change

In this chapter, we present results from the literature search by characterizing the 549 relevant documents. We present data on definitions of organizational culture and of key drivers of organizational culture change and policy recommendations based on that literature. Finally, we describe our process of vetting the literature review findings with a panel of experts.

Literature Review

Most of the documents that we included addressed organizational culture (87 percent): 488 documents (74 percent) were about organizational culture only, 71 were about climate only (13 percent), and 70 were about both culture and climate (13 percent).

Document Type: Design and Data Collection Approach

Slightly more than half of the documents were empirical in nature (55 percent), most of which were observational studies (48 percent). Another 26 documents (5 percent) reported findings from longitudinal studies. Only 13 documents (2 percent) used robust designs based on experimental or quasiexperimental designs. In terms of data collection methods, among the 330 empirical documents, 42.7 percent used qualitative methods, 39.7 percent used quantitative methods, and the remaining 17.6 percent used mixed methods.

After closer examination of the 39 articles that used more robust designs (26 longitudinal and 13 experimental), we identified some of the key factors that influenced organizational culture change. Examples of articles in our literature review with robust designs include one that used a randomized trial of an organizational intervention with community-based mental health programs and clinicians serving youth (Glisson, et al., 2012), and another that used a pre-post survey design to assess change in attitudes among parole officers and supervisors over a six-month period (Schlager, 2008). These documents provided some important general lessons about organizational culture change. First, although leadership is one of the most commonly described ingredients for achieving cultural transformation, organizational values may remain stable over time and can be difficult to change even when environmental pressures are motivating change (Campbell, 2004). However, the process of change is complex and not quick, and even when cultural transformation is achieved, it may take up to three years (Munroe, Kaza, and Howard, 2011). This literature also suggests that when change takes place, generally with dedicated transformational leadership and through formal and large-scale training and organizational development/learning interventions, it can be sustained for more than a year (Simpson, Joe, and Rowan-Szal, 2007). Having a dynamic design process, changing what is not working and focusing on what works well, along with attending to everyday relationships and behaviors are also highlighted in this subset of documents (Cottingham et al., 2008). Most of these studies evaluated multicomponent interventions, suggesting that a program of change is needed and that any single factor may be insufficient, a finding reflected in other literature reviews (see Fernandez and Rainey's 2006 overview of the change literature, Burke's 2014 review of the climate and culture change literature, or the principles of alignment discussed by Bowen and Ostroff [2004] and Ehrhart, Schneider, and Macey [2014]). In sum, change is difficult to achieve, it may take a long time, and it may take a combination of strategies operating at multiple levels for success.

Type of Industry

Figure 3.1 shows the distribution of all 549 documents by type of industry. Most of the documents were from the health/medical or corporate sectors (29 percent and

Figure 3.1
Documents by Industry

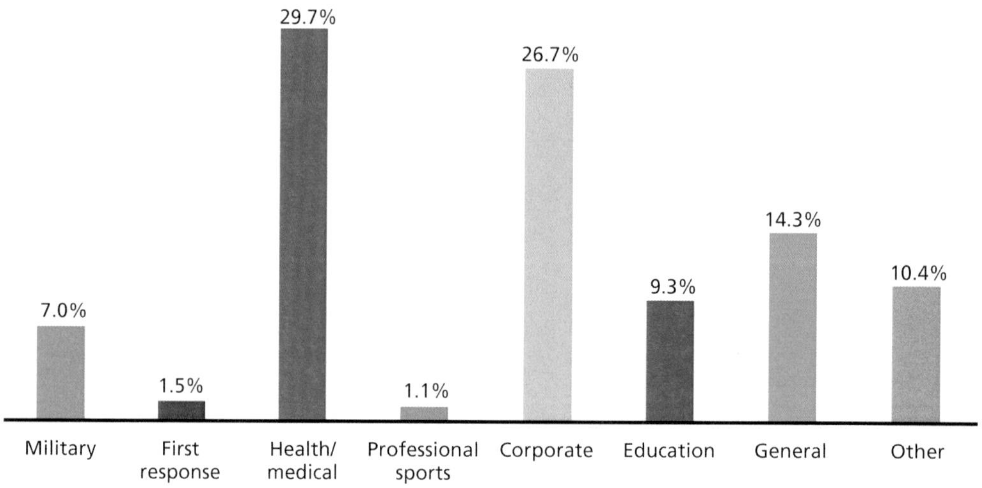

RAND *RR1588-3.1*

27 percent, respectively). Few documents were obtained from the first response or sports sectors.

Subcultures

We included a review of subcultures because of the importance of leadership's consistent and passionate communication of priorities. If subordinates know the goals, then they will not be left to their own assumptions, which could ultimately lead to differing subcultures (Schein, 2004). Moreover, as the Army is a large and diverse organization, subcultures should be an issue of consideration for climate and culture change efforts. In our review, we found a limited amount of documents that discuss various subcultures. Of only 66, 35 were of general content and 26 were domain-specific. Only 27 of the documents were empirically based, and only one used a robust longitudinal design. Most of the documents were coded as having ambiguous information about the presence or description of particular subcultures. Where we did identify information about a subculture, 17 documents addressed a counterculture (i.e., clash between an electronic data systems culture and business development culture in an organization), five addressed an enhancing subculture (i.e., a flexible learning culture to enhance reporting culture), and five addressed an orthogonal subculture (i.e., importance of both separateness and integration).

Table 3.1 provides some example excerpts from documents to illustrate each of the three types of subcultures for both general and domain-specific documents.

Table 3.1
Examples of Subculture Content for General and Domain-Specific Documents

Subculture	General	Domain-Specific
Counter	Dynamics of multiple, sometimes competing subcultures within organizations (Hofstede, 1998, and Wilson, 1989, as cited in Dull, 2010, p. 861)	(1) Different subcultures can exist throughout an organization, and (2) members of each subculture hold different attitudes toward corporate sustainability which are distinct from that of other subcultures (Linnenluecke and Griffiths, 2010)
Enhancing	Find the best subculture and hold it up as an example (Kingshott, 2009, p. 65)	Reporting subculture; just subculture; flexible subculture; learning subculture (Ruchlin, et al., 2004)
Orthogonal	Executives should acknowledge the need for subcultures and carefully examine the balance of separateness and integration that works best for the whole company (Kampas, 2003)	The intent of the academy was to have distinct faculty groups (rotators, permanent military, and civilians) with strengths, experiences, and expertise that were unique from and complementary to each other (Ruvolo, 2007)

NOTE: See Appendix B for full citations.

Unit of Analysis

We also looked at whether there are differences by unit of analysis. Among the documents that included information on unit of analysis (n=401), the vast majority addressed the organization as the unit (n=294). Fifty-two documents addressed smaller groups (e.g., military units/teams), and 45 addressed the individual as the unit of analysis. Twenty documents addressed other units, such as an entire region, a state, or a nation. We looked at how the 20 drivers identified in the literature review map out across levels of analysis.

Content

As far as broad culture change mechanisms coded during the document abstraction, we found that among those with mechanisms coded (41 percent were inapplicable), most of the documents discussed either training or mentoring (34 percent). Monitoring and control was discussed in 17 percent of the documents, and another 8 percent discussed selection.

Based on our coding of the literature content, we found that nearly all documents covered values, attitudes, and beliefs (n=476; 88 percent). Documents also commonly addressed norms (n=375; 69 percent), followed by knowledge, skills, and resources (n=232; 43 percent). Symbols were less common in the literature, with only 91 documents including such content (17 percent). In terms of outcomes discussed, the most common types were behavioral outcomes (n=385; 71 percent) and psychological outcomes (n=307; 57 percent). Some 232 of the documents (43 percent) covered social outcomes, and only 79 documents (15 percent) dealt with financial outcomes.

Definitions of Organizational Culture

There are many different ways to think about organizational culture, so a clear definition will help guide efforts at implementation. Definitions provide scope, target areas, and an opportunity to bring relevant stakeholders together to develop a central goal that will enable consideration of interventions that are appropriately targeted and agreed upon, which is of vital importance when dealing with constructs like culture that are shared across the organization. We examined how culture is defined in the literature to develop ways of thinking through definitional issues.

The literature review identified 369 documents that listed definition(s) of organizational culture or climate (of the 549 documents coded). Among these 369 documents, 69 percent covered culture only, 17 percent covered climate only, and 15 percent covered both culture and climate. We show the distribution of definitions by domain and industry in Table 3.2. Among these definitions, about 45 percent (n=167) were domain specific, while the remaining were general. Overall, more of the definitions came from the medical (28 percent) and corporate fields (25 percent), while the fewest were from military literature (last column of Table 3.2).

Table 3.2
Number and Percentage of Definitions by Domain and Sector

Sector	Domain-specific n	Domain-specific Definitions %	General Definitions n	General Definitions %	All Definitions n	All Definitions %
Military	12	7	14	7	26	7
Corporate	52	31	39	19	91	25
Education	12	7	23	11	35	9
Medical	41	25	62	31	103	28
General	30	18	39	19	69	19
Others	20	12	24	12	45	12
Total	167	100	201	100	369	100

The frequency of distribution of general definitions followed this same trend. The percentage of domain-specific definitions by industry ranged from 7 to 31 percent, with the lowest relative percentage in the education (7 percent) and military (7 percent) literatures and the highest percentages in the medical (25 percent) and corporate industry literature (31 percent). The domain-specific definitions include definitions of ethical culture, safety culture, inclusive culture, blame-free culture, tough culture, organizational learning culture, etc. For example, an inclusive culture is one where individuals of all backgrounds experience a sense of belonging and experience their uniqueness as valued (Military Leadership Diversity Commission, 2011), and a safety culture is the product of individual and group values, attitudes, competencies, and patterns of behavior that determine the commitment to an organization's health and safety programs (Great Britain Health and Safety Commission, 1993; Meaney, 2004).

Within the general definitions of culture category, we identified 86 unique definitions.[1] A few were cited multiple times by other publications. For example, 73 articles cite Schein's definitions of culture. Schein's specific definition appears in 30 articles:

> Culture is a pattern of shared basic assumptions, invented, discovered, or developed by a given group as it learns to cope with its problems of external adaptation and internal integration that has worked well enough to be considered valid, and, therefore, is to be taught to new members of the group as the correct way to perceive, think, and feel in relation to those problems' reframing. (Schein, 1990)

[1] Note that some documents cited more than one definition and some definitions were cited repeatedly across documents. Also, popular authors in the field published variants on definitions across sources, making the exact count of unique definitions uncertain.

Sixty-six percent of documents focused at a deep level (e.g., emphasizing assumptions, values, attitudes, beliefs), relative to 6 percent that focused on the surface level and 27 percent that examined both deep and surface levels. About 9 percent of definitions purported a top-down approach; 24 percent purported both a top-down (strategic socialization by leaders) and bottom-up (shared values, perceptions, or daily interactions) approach, and none explicitly purported a bottom-up approach (66 percent did not contain sufficient information to make a determination). In terms of receptivity, 6 percent of definitions communicated openness to change, 3 percent were resistant to change, and 91 percent could not be coded. The full listing of unique definitions with source information and coding results is provided in Appendix C. Table 3.3 shows the distribution of the 86 unique general definitions for the additional coding on level of depth, development, and receptivity (see Appendix A for operational definitions). To summarize, we identified a wide variety of definitions, suggesting little overall consistency. However, many of the more heavily cited definitions shared some key features. These included the idea of shared assumptions (beliefs, norms, values, ideas, etc.) by groups and underlying patterns of an organization.

Drivers of Organizational Change

The literature reflects 20 categories of key drivers of organizational culture and climate change. These drivers and their descriptions appear in Table 3.4. Although we confined our literature search to organizational culture and climate change as described previously rather than widening the aperture to include the more general organizational change and development literature, the drivers revealed resemble those discussed in the more general literature (see Burke, 2002, or the change steps discussed by Fernandez and Rainey, 2006). Figure 3.2 shows that among these drivers, we found that organizational openness to transformation was the most prevalent (126 documents), followed by communication (107 documents) and collaboration (85 documents). The least prevalent drivers were autonomy (14 documents), standardization (19 documents), and mentoring (also 19 documents).

Table 3.3
Characteristics of the 86 Unique General Definitions

Level of Depth	n	%	Development	n	%	Receptivity	n	%
Deep	57	66	Top-down	8	9	Open	5	6
Surface	5	6	Bottom-up	0	0	Resistant	3	3
Deep and surface	23	27	Top-down and bottom-up	21	24	Unclear	78	91
Unclear	1	1	Unclear	57	66			
Total	86	100	Total	86	100	Total	86	100

Regardless of the unit of analysis, transformation, communication, and collaboration were all among the five most prevalent drivers. For documents that addressed the organization as the unit, training and incentives were also commonly addressed. Documents addressing smaller groups (units/teams) commonly addressed resources and measurement, and in documents addressing individuals, alignment and stakeholders were among the top five.

Table 3.4
Coding Categories for Drivers and Policy Recommendations

Name	Description
Accountability	Underscores shared responsibilities and accountability
Autonomy	Allows for autonomy
Collaboration	Uses shared decisionmaking, collaboration, teamwork, cross-functionality
Communication	Uses clear, open, transparent communication, etc.
Fit	Has values congruent with personnel (shared values, norms, symbols) or individual alignment with organization (person-organization fit)
Goals	Sets goals; uses coherent planning, persistence, and strategic/inspirational/ innovative thinking; results oriented
Incentives	Applies incentives, encouragement, motivation, or rewards
Measurement	Tracks progress through performance measurement, audit and feedback, gap analysis, benchmarking, Plan-Do-Study-Act cycles, change documentation/ reporting systems, etc.
Mentoring	Employs mentoring, role modeling, or coaching
Resolution	Emphasizes problem-solving, error and disagreement resolution, tolerance for risk, surfacing/examining underlying assumptions, mindfulness, and self-awareness
Resources	Devotes sufficient resources (financial, staffing, time, etc.) to change efforts
Selection	Selects/retains appropriate personnel
Socialization	Is people-centered (values social interaction, socialization)
Stakeholders	Engages stakeholders, includes diverse perspectives, or develops partnerships
Standardization	Systematizes recommendations in day-to-day operations and standards
Structure	Has a structure/infrastructure that enables change (physical environment, size, spatial dynamics)
Training	Develops personnel through training (skills, engagement, education, etc.)
Transformation	Promotes openness to change/transformation, flexibility, adaptability, optimism, or learning orientation
Trust	Focuses on trust, empowerment, self-efficacy, etc.
Vision	Articulates a clear mission, clear vision/goals, and clear expectations/expectation management

Figure 3.2
Prevalence of Drivers in the Literature

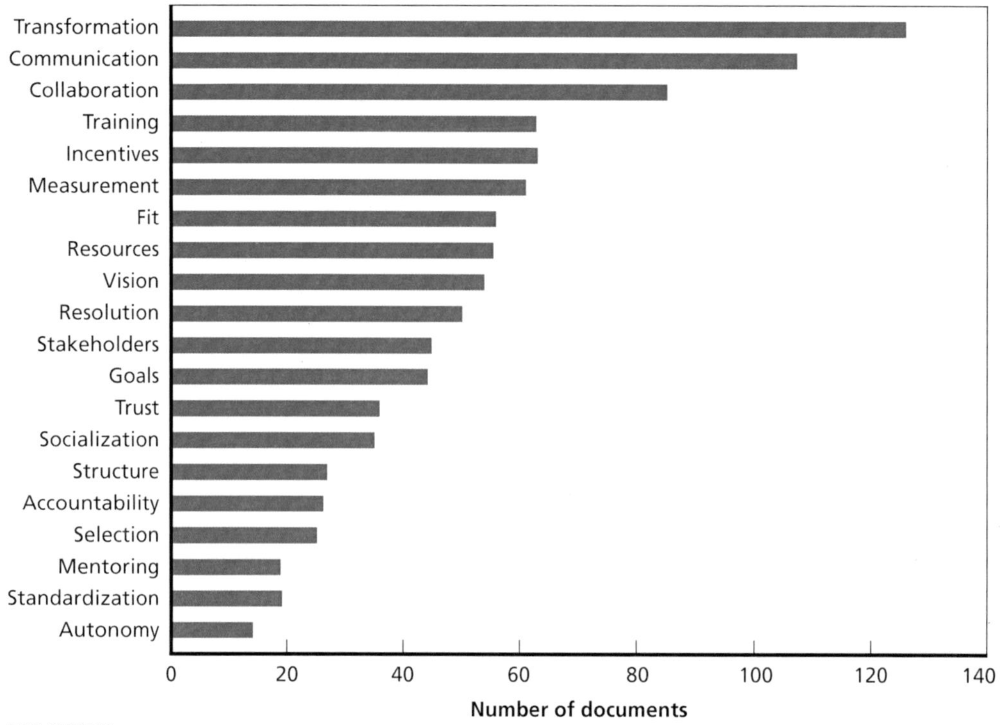

RAND *RR1588-3.2*

To place some of these drivers in context, we provide examples for those identified as more prevalent. For example, Army high-level leadership could exemplify "transformation" by emphasizing the importance of prompt mental health care through campaigns to eliminate stigma and programs to educate mid-level leaders to identify troops who need help and get them treatment without career repercussions. High-level leaders, as well as leaders at all levels, could also publicly talk about their own struggles with behavioral health issues and set an example by getting assistance for these issues.

"Communication" is also important in that clear, consistent communication is necessary across levels of command. For example, even one contravening narrative regarding requirements that soldiers' careers go hold while they receive treatment will throw the validity of efforts combating stigma into doubt, so it is vital for this type of effort for the communication to be consistent and authentic. A "communication" driver may therefore include initiatives to reduce potential negative consequences of reporting. For example, policies that preclude individuals from carrying out particular duties if they are getting mental health care should be reviewed regularly and communicated widely.

"Collaboration" is the third most important driver. Discussion of strategies as they are implemented at various levels in a collaborative manner, using the input of stakeholders at the various levels to make this implementation feasible, and incorporating messages into the existing training culture of the Army would also be important drivers of organizational culture change. As noted, communication must be with one voice, so a collaborative determination of strategy in which leaders at all levels can engage may make for a more cohesive implementation.

We did not observe much variation in terms of outcomes across drivers. For all drivers, with a few exceptions, behavioral outcomes were the most commonly mentioned. Many drivers—goals, stakeholders, standardization, training, resources, autonomy, and selection—also mentioned psychological and social outcomes approximately equally or slightly less. Few documents, regardless of type of driver, measured financial outcomes.

The heat map in Figure 3.3 shows the percentage of documents across the different industries to illuminate issues of feasibility differentiation across fields, with a darker color in a cell indicating a higher percentage of documents. Despite not being chosen as one of the key drivers for Army implementation, "transformation" is nonetheless common in all fields, including the military, as is "communication." "Goals" did not figure highly in any industry category, as shown by the consistently pale hue,

Figure 3.3
Percentage of Documents Mentioning Drivers by Industry

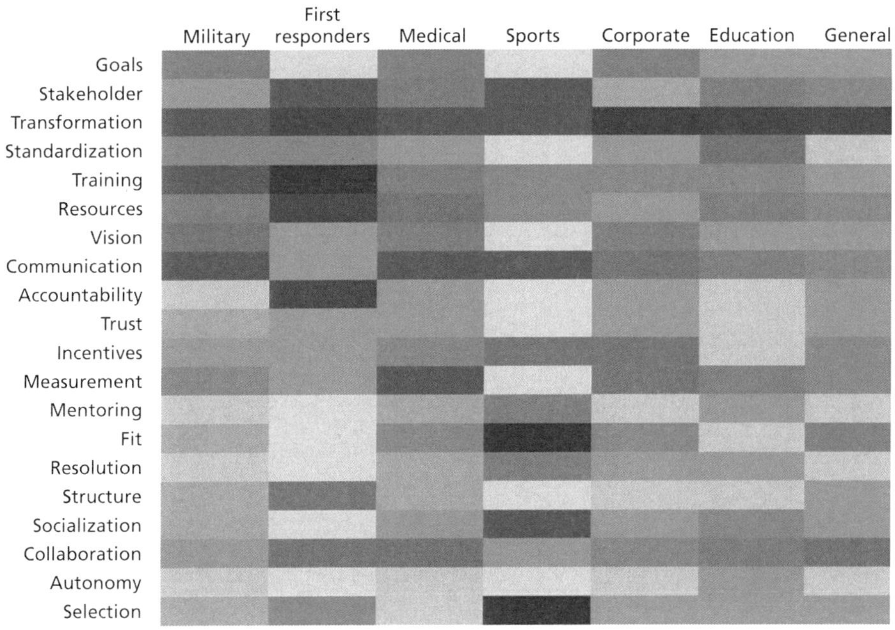

and "accountability" figured only for first responders. "Training" was discussed at length, and it also appears with relative frequency in the military literature. Therefore, although the literature did show some differentiation in terms of types of efforts investigated for given contexts, no set of drivers appears unique to the military context. Rather, drivers appeared to be both general in nature and generally considered regardless of the specific type of organization. Our panelist ratings therefore provide potential insight into applicability to the Army context.

Within each type of subculture, we observed a different pattern of drivers. For those identifying a counterculture, the most commonly mentioned drivers in the literature were measurement, collaboration, and communication. In contrast, accountability and transformation were the most commonly mentioned drivers from the subset of literature that identified orthogonal subcultures, although communication was also mentioned (as it was for countercultures). For enhancing cultures, training and goals stood out as being more common relative to other drivers.

SME Panel

Pre-Conference Driver Ratings

We obtained feedback from panelists about each of the 20 drivers to place the literature findings within a military context. In Figure 3.4, we summarize panelist ratings made before the in-person discussion (the averages across all six panelists). We sorted the drivers by the sum of the ratings for alignment of Army mission and feasibility of implementing change. Although the range was greater for feasibility (averaged ratings ranged from a low of two to a high of four) than alignment (where averaged ratings ranged from a low of three to a high of 4.8), SME agreement was generally fairly high across the drivers. For both alignment and feasibility, driver rating standard deviations were rarely greater than one. Some exceptions included "mentoring" and "structure" for alignment ratings and "measurement," "collaboration," and "structure" for feasibility ratings.[2] In summary, most of the drivers align with the Army, but there was far more variability for feasibility.

We list the five top-rated drivers with the definitions for each in Table 3.5. These five top-rated drivers include only one of the five most prevalent drivers (training) based on the literature review prevalence ordering in Figure 3.2. We discussed all of the drivers at least briefly during the panel, but given time constraints were forced to focus more deeply on only a few and use them to elicit wider-ranging discussion.

[2] Based on discussion, it seemed like the consistency for the rating of "structure" might have been based on difficulty envisioning how that particular driver would be implemented in the Army as it related to physical setting (note that a meta-analysis of organizational development interventions in public and private organizations, for example, found relatively few examples that fit a similar categorization; Robertson and Seneviratne, 1995).

The panelists agreed these five drivers are both well aligned with the Army mission and feasible for the Army to target as levers for culture change, based on pre-conference thought processes. "Fit" reflects the Army's emphasis on mission and the fact that, as an all-volunteer force, it can anticipate that individuals who join have some knowledge of that mission and desire to serve. "Training" reflects the extensive training system that the Army uses to develop its professionals throughout their careers and the Army's reliance on training to distribute information about what it means to be in the Army. As we will see, setting strategic "goals" and then supporting them with tactical "goals" aligns with the Army way of doing business, as well. (In contrast, "allowing for autonomy" was seen as less aligned in general with the Army mission and less feasible, as well.) "Vision" is about clearly articulating the Army's mission and goals to set expectations. Finally, "trust," empowerment, and self-efficacy are important for the Army to facilitate performance and the mission.

We used these pre-conference driver ratings to generate discussion at the SME panel. We discussed those drivers that seemed to be considered most aligned and feasible—the "top five." We also discussed areas where ratings were similar and where they were different, and whether anything seemed missing. Based on that discussion,

Figure 3.4
Summary of Panelist Pre-Conference Ratings Across Drivers

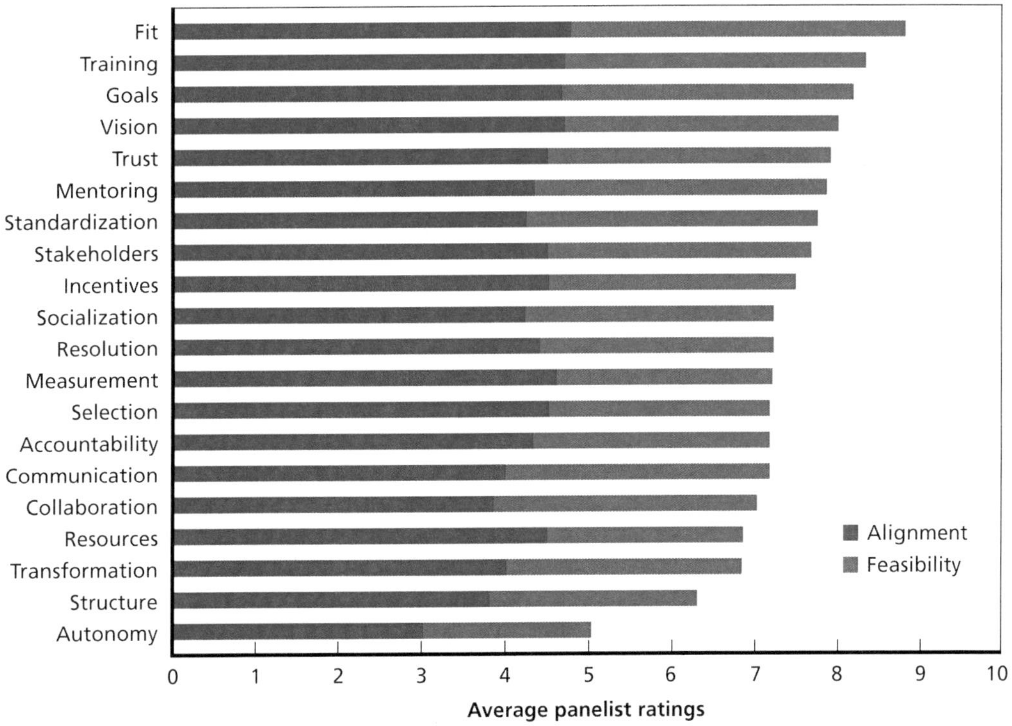

RAND *RR1588-3.4*

Table 3.5
Top-Rated Drivers and Descriptions from Pre-Conference Ratings

Name	Description
Fit	Has values congruent with personnel (shared values, norms, symbols) or individual alignment with organization (person-organization fit)
Training	Develops personnel through training (skills, engagement, education, etc.)
Goals	Sets goals, uses coherent planning, persistence, and strategic/inspirational/innovative thinking; results oriented
Vision	Articulates a clear mission, clear vision/goals, and clear expectations/expectation management
Trust	Focuses on trust, empowerment, self-efficacy, etc.

NOTE: These are excerpted here for convenience; the drivers in their entirety are shown in Table 2.1.

we came to consensus that it was important to include two additional drivers not originally included in our list: (1) engaging both formal and informal leaders and (2) understanding current culture. The first is important because, although we identified a driver from the literature that encompassed stakeholder engagement, we felt that given the hierarchical character of the Army, the role of informal leaders should be highlighted beyond a general exhortation to include diverse perspectives. The second is important because the literature on change implementation sometimes assumes that change agents make a cultural or climate diagnosis before initiation of the change effort (Armenakis, Harris, and Feild, 2001; Schein, 2004; Schneider, Ehrhart, and Macey, 2011). However, we felt it was such a necessary aspect that specifying its presence was a requirement, although it cannot strictly be considered a driver. We further address this issue below.

SME Discussion Integrated with the Literature: Process Recommendations and Targeted Drivers

SMEs first agreed on an approach for how to achieve institutional culture change and arrived at a consensus on which of the more than 20 drivers of organizational culture change to prioritize. With respect to achieving organizational culture change, the panel recommended a holistic approach (rather than a crisis-response approach). A holistic approach requires active consideration of the overlaps in different drivers of change and initiatives that target them and how they can work together or might conflict for a given culture change effort. The research supports this aligned approach (Ford and Foster-Fishman, 2012; see also Burke, 2014; Fernandez and Rainey, 2006; Ostroff, Kinicki, and Muhammad, 2012). A holistic approach would be aligned so that drivers would not conflict with each other and would serve to create a strong situation.

That is, it is important to send a clear message about what is valued within an organization across multiple policies, practices, and reward systems (Bowen and Ostroff, 2004).

The literature also emphasizes holism in the sense of using multiple drivers to effect successful change, though specific empirical prescriptions on how many and what kinds of coordinating efforts are required are not available.

As an example of overlap, SMEs discussed how "accountability" overlaps with the roles played by leaders in the Army to develop their subordinates through "training," another driver. Determining how best to hold leaders accountable for subordinate development and enabling both leaders and subordinates to commit and learn from mistakes, is an example of a holistic approach. However, the discussion also made clear that a holistic understanding of all Army culture is perhaps not entirely feasible. Hence, it is worthwhile to point out that not all aspects of climate and culture will be relevant (e.g., Schein's 2004 discussion on the impracticability of knowing and understanding *every* aspect of a culture before implementing a culture change effort).

Another example of the necessity of coordinating drivers is the broader tension within the Army between discipline and autonomous behavior. Discipline is essential to the military mission, and certain behavioral strictures are required to enforce it; however, the concept of the "strategic sergeant" suggests that even at low ranks, military members need to be developed as thoughtful decisionmakers who can be trusted to act in an ethical manner.

In keeping with this general frame to the discussion, we determined a general outline would help put the drivers into a context in which they could be better considered for implementation.

General Framework for Approaching a Culture Problem

Panelists suggested that as a first step, it is critical to determine that there is a problem and identify what it is (see also Schein, 2004).

1. **Define the problem.**
2. **Understand current culture,** particularly in relation to a problem but at a general enough level to enable a holistic course of action.
3. **Define/articulate the desired culture or vision.** Note that "vision" is the level at which senior leaders would engage with the problem. Such a definition would be similar to the Australian Army's "Statement of Cultural Intent," which was articulated before an extensive years-long culture change effort and is now a priority second only to supporting personnel and operations. Another way to define the desired vision would be seeking what a panelist called a "Culture of Trust."
4. **Identify specific goals.** Note that "goals" is the level at which operational/tactical implementation–level leaders would engage with the problem.

For any problem, a holistic approach that targets drivers in a coordinated fashion also facilitates change that is more likely to persist. Panelists contrasted this approach with the crisis-response approach, in which a given problem area is supplanted by a subsequent crisis; the original problem crops up again because it has not been addressed in a comprehensive fashion. Although manifestations may change, the underlying issues remain and are not conclusively solved. The panelists discussed the issue of treatment of women in the services as an example of a crisis-response approach, exemplified by recurrent sexual assault and harassment scandals. Schein (2004) notes that scandals may be used as a tool in change efforts: A situation can be used to highlight relevant assumptions and norms and provide evidence that there is a discrepancy between how these are spoken of and documented compared with how they are implemented in reality. However, whereas scandals may have their uses for change efforts, our panelists did not indicate that crisis response typically engenders calm and thoughtful responses and coordinated culture change.

While panel discussion produced these specific steps, they are certainly consistent with recommendations in the literature (including those by Burke, 2002; Fernandez and Rainey, 2006; Kotter, 1995; and Schein, 2004). Also, some general principles should be followed in attempting to institute cultural change in the Army, as the panel concluded.

The first is a need for clarity and specificity. When approaching culture change, one panelist noted that research supports focusing on specific behavior sets (e.g., Burke, 2014; Schein, 2004), and climate in particular is quite often conceived of as a certain type of climate (e.g., "safety climate," "climate of fear"). If the problem is articulated with concrete examples and detailed definitions, groups can more easily come to a common understanding of the problem and the desired solution—and because culture and climate are group constructs, a common understanding is vital. Moreover, measuring changes in behaviors (which can be observed and tracked) is much more feasible than changing values and assumptions. Burke (2014) suggests that behavior change (and subsequent culture change) can occur, for example, through the modeling of specific behaviors by leadership in a top-down manner. Finally, framing change efforts within the parameters of a certain problem behavior helps leaders articulate a common definition and goal set for culture and climate change.

It is also essential to engage people at different levels of an organization (see also Burke, 2002; Schneider, Ehrhart, and Macey, 2011) through cascading discussions of expected behaviors and accountability and to understand that different drivers will respond in different timelines (immediately, in the short term, or over the longer term). These aspects need to be taken into account for realistic planning. In addition, clear and consistent communication across all levels of leadership is important for maximizing the alignment and effectiveness of change.

Below, we summarize the consensus discussion regarding which drivers from the literature demonstrate the most promise for culture or climate change in the context of the Army. We focus on the five drivers most frequently nominated to panelists' "top three" and on examples drawn from the discussion to put a finer point on how best to implement these drivers in the Army. We also bolster the discussion with the literature itself. We cite some specific examples of overlap in the discussion below; note that such overlap is typical rather than exceptional. The tabular summary provided to the panelists for their feedback is reproduced in its entirety in Appendix E. Table 3.6 provides an overview of the key drivers and their longer descriptions. These top five drivers include only two of the five most prevalent drivers ("goals" and "training") based on pre-conference ratings of alignment and feasibility. Thus, some new drivers were introduced during discussion of the gathered panelists as ultimately being more useful than originally thought based on panelists' pre-conference individual ratings. That is, discussion of application to the Army from a variety of perspectives generated three other drivers that were ultimately more important for consideration: **accountability**, **resources**, and **engagement**.

The most important driver was **Goals.** In terms of the discussion, this was seen as part of the typical work of the Army—subordinate leaders take commanders' intent and translate that at lower levels, often with specific and more tactical goals. In the Army, senior leaders' goal is in effect to describe the general "vision," as called for in many implementation recommendations in the literature (Fernandez and Rainey, 2006; Kotter, 1995; Schein, 2004). Subordinate leaders then take their commanders' intent and break it down into specific goals implementable at the relevant level of authority. The original vision must be clear enough that definitional ambiguities do not result in implementation that contravenes the intent. However, given the variety of different subcultures in an organization as large and diverse as the Army, local autonomy is required to be able to interpret commander intent in tandem with unique subcultural issues. An example might be senior leaders' goal/vision of "fostering an innovative culture" to increase creative problem solving. U.S. Army Training and Doctrine Command may interpret that vision by creating a unit like the Asymmetric Warfare Group, which can provide training to help soldiers innovate and adapt effectively against adversaries in complex environments. At the brigade command level, the goal

Table 3.6
Key Drivers and Descriptions for Army Change

Drivers	Description
Goals	Setting goals; coherent planning; persistence; strategic, inspirational, innovative thinking; results oriented
Accountability	Underscoring shared responsibilities and accountability
Training	Developing personnel through training (skills, engagement, education)
Resources	Devoting sufficient resources (finances, staff, time) to change
Engagement	Engaging both formal and informal leaders (stakeholders)

NOTE: These are excerpted here for convenience; the drivers in their entirety are shown in Table 3.4.

may be to foster innovative tactical problem solving; a brigade commander may send soldiers to courses that foster innovation and problem solving and provide support for innovative ideas. Junior soldiers can internalize innovation by observing leaders at each level encouraging innovation and through creative problem solving incorporated into unit training. (Note that setting goals should be inextricably linked with measurement of progress toward those goals.)

The second most important driver was **Accountability.** The panel considered this to be a key part of "leadership," and at least one panelist specified that other leadership-type responsibilities (and drivers from the literature), such as developing personnel/training and role modeling/mentoring, were subordinate to the overarching driver of accountability, given that developing quality Army personnel is often an explicit part of job responsibilities. The discussion generated several aspects of accountability in the context of the Army.

One noted point was that it could be difficult in the Army context to give and receive the honest feedback needed to enable accountability (this issue is hardly Army specific; see Newman, Kinney, Farr, 2003, and discussion of feedback interventions for organizational development in Church, Walker, Brockner, 2002). When a behavior change is sought, in some cases undesired behaviors should be expected and seen as learning opportunities for honest feedback. Zero error tolerance is an unforgiving standard that may cause people to game the reporting system rather than truly change behavior.

Part of accountability is also measuring the desired outcome, essential to tracking and measuring change (see Armenakis, Harris, and Feild, 2001; Burke, 2014; Fernandez and Rainey, 2006; Kotter, 1995). Schein's (2004) embedding mechanisms also consider what organizational leaders measure, and he notes that measurement in itself sends a signal about leader priorities. When carefully considered in the context of holistic change, these signals facilitate alignment. It is easier to focus on and measure desired behavioral changes. In the Army context, an increase in traffic at a behavioral health clinic might be one measurement of a desired outcome. Another measurement of a desired outcome would be a drop in the more critical consequences of behavioral health challenges (for example, more people might seek treatment before becoming dependent on substance abuse to self-manage PTSD). A third outcome might be surveys that show decreased perceptions of stigma for seeking mental health treatment, although this is a less direct measurement. Measuring the desired outcome enables leaders to determine whether they are correctly prioritizing a given goal.

Appropriate measurement also requires an understanding of current culture and climate, a thorough definitional effort, and realistic estimates of expected change, particularly when behaviors that are targeted are quite low in terms of base rate. Armenakis, Harris, and Feild (2001) discuss what change would and should look like; surveys may show that an undesirable behavior is noted as "frequent" both before and after a change effort because after a change, respondents may have a lower anchor for what frequency is appropriate.

Finally, part of accountability is *actual execution of existing policy*. Some issues relevant to the context of gender integration are as yet unarticulated in policy; however, ink has likely been spent on the specifics of other relevant issues in terms of policy guidance as well as pertinent outcome variables. What is missing is actual implementation. In some cases, determining and setting realistic priorities among competing imperatives is a challenge to leadership that must be addressed as well.

The third most frequently nominated driver was **Training**, which includes quite a broad purview. Our panelists noted that the military makes much use of training, but it may not be sufficient to facilitate organizational culture change. Schein (2004) discusses that training can help create the psychological safety to enable change; if change requires new skill sets, these skills must be taught to alleviate targets' concerns about new performance requirements. Armenakis, Harris, and Feild (2001) note that training is one of the human resource levers that may be engaged in culture change efforts, and they describe its use both in terms of teaching new knowledge, skills, and abilities and in terms of reinforcing messages for an overall change effort. Peer and supervisor support helps ensure that training is applied in the workplace. Opportunities to practice soon after training and reorganizing work flow so that trained behaviors are integrated into regular processes also help (see reviews by Brown and Sitzmann, 2011; Burke and Hutchins, 2007).

Panelists discussed the importance of tailoring training to particular subgroups, especially given competing demands and limited resources. An example was to consider training to a specific problem behavior rather than all possible negative behaviors. Training to tiers would target high-level leaders with one form of training; leaders can then lead by example (enforce and model); Burke (2002) notes that training interventions for organizational culture change are most often targeted specifically at senior leaders. Another approach is creating modules that can be deployed only where relevant (though the definition of relevance should be carefully considered). For example, if women are embedded in a given unit, gender diversity training is key; if not, different training may have a somewhat higher prioritization. Note here the phrase "somewhat higher," as consideration of the issue reveals that even men in an entirely male unit have to interact with women.

Resources were also high on panelists' list of nomination and are related to the provision of training. General implementation guidance highlights this as well (e.g., Fernandez and Rainey, 2006; Kotter, 1995), as does Schein (2004) in his discussion of embedding mechanisms. Certainly, measuring outcomes, enforcing accountability, and establishing training all require resources; target participation in these efforts likewise requires organizational resources. Resourcing efforts adequately also demonstrates that efforts are a priority. Pursuing holistic change implies a variety of efforts, thoughtfully aligned and with sufficient resources to carry them out. Time and attention are limited, so it is important to plan for the worst in provision of resources rather than hope that people will simply find the time and effort required.

Leadership is often emphasized in culture change or organizational change more generally (e.g., Burke, 2002; Burke, 2014; Day, Griffin, and Louw, 2014; Schein, 2004; Schneider, Ehrhart, and Macey, 2011), although the literature varies in how a "leader" is defined and can encompass everyone from company CEO to line supervisors to change champions who may or may not hold a formal position. Another driver noted prominently by our panel was a write-in suggestion that **targeting formal *and informal* leaders** was an important factor in influencing change. Targeting is in some sense included in our ratings (e.g., the driver "engages stakeholders, includes diverse perspectives, or develops partnerships"). For example, one article (Hauck, Winsett, and Kuric, 2013) about promoting a safety culture within hospital surgery units noted the importance of registered nurses who moved around the hospital and had the most interaction with various units. These nurses had the strongest effects on safety culture at follow-up and were seen as crucial change agents. However, targeting *informal* leaders—early adopters and influencers—was considered important enough to highlight separately. Depending on the circumstance, informal leaders may include first sergeants, chaplains, and similar people with specific authority, as well as other influencers without any official formally granted authority, job, or rank. Those who volunteer to be change champions may also be included here. (Formal leaders are generally readily identifiable in the military hierarchy.)

Overall Summary of SME Panel

Our panelists suggested that the prevalence of a given driver in the literature does not necessarily indicate its appropriateness for the Army or its potential for success. As one noted, management literature can be swayed by fads; a heavy concentration on transformational leadership may be one such example. In our coding of the policy recommendations and drivers, we noted that the term "transformational leadership" seemed almost a touchstone. However, some reviewed articles spoke of it in generalities rather than providing specific prescriptions regarding how transformational leadership behaviors helped generate culture change. Moreover, many reviews (Fernandez and Rainey, 2006; Martins, 2011; Ostroff, Kinicki, and Muhammad, 2012; Schneider, Ehrhart, and Macey, 2011) indicate that little research has provided specific implementation guidance supported by a rigorous evidence base despite notable interest in transformational leadership.

Based on the discussion of our coding categories, as well as the summary of the panel discussion, the panel delved quite deeply into the issues surrounding certain drivers and perhaps interpreted them a bit idiosyncratically. That does not detract from the importance of the panelists' observations, but does explain some discrepancies. Our panelists and the literature are in agreement on key points, however—developing appropriate culture/climate definition and problem diagnosis; articulating a change vision that is detailed enough even at its greatest breadth to generate actionable tactical goals; taking a holistic approach, with multiple drivers and change mechanisms; and engaging at multiple organizational levels.

CHAPTER FOUR

Findings and Recommendations

In this chapter, we briefly summarize our main findings and suggest recommended actions for Army leadership and the military more broadly where applicable. Our recommendations may help craft culture change efforts, implemented at whatever levels are appropriate, to help servicemembers and leaders embrace the many changes taking place. However, our recommendations are framed quite broadly, and Army leaders would need to adjust these recommendations to a specific context to use them in a change implementation effort. Interested readers may read Chapter Three for more specific examples and discussion.

Findings

Our literature review led to several findings. For this overview, we organize these conclusions according to our guiding questions:

1. How is organizational culture defined?
2. What drives/maintains particular cultures or subcultures?
3. How can we apply promising approaches to institutional change from a variety of industries to the Army?

Definitions of Organizational Culture

Among the 86 unique definitions we identified from the literature, eight use a top-down approach (which may best resonate with military hierarchy), 57 convey deep (as opposed to surface) content, and five communicate openness to change. These unique definitions are also sufficiently general to apply to the Army. Future definitions targeting organizational culture change should focus on incorporating the following components:

- Emphasis on deep culture (assumptions, values, attitudes, beliefs) rather than on surface culture (symbols)

- Receptivity to change
- Both bottom-up (arising from members' shared values) and top-down (strategic socialization) approaches to developing change.

Our first recommendation below discusses in greater detail our recommendations regarding definitional requirements.

Drivers of Organizational Culture and Climate Change

We identified 20 types of drivers of organizational culture/climate change from the literature. Several align particularly well with the existing Army culture and are feasible within the military structure. The top five drivers relevant to the Army are as follows:

1. **Goals:** Articulate and set clear goals; use coherent planning, persistence, and strategic, inspirational, innovative thinking; results oriented
2. **Accountability:** Underscore shared responsibilities and accountability
3. **Training:** Develop personnel through training (skills, engagement, etc.), education
4. **Resources:** Devote sufficient resources (financial, staffing, time, etc.) to change efforts
5. **Targeting:** Target both formal and informal leaders (engage stakeholders).

These top drivers are not intended to be viewed or implemented in isolation given how difficult it is to change an organization. It is expected that a combination of these (and other) strategies may be necessary for success. First and foremost, the Army senior leadership must understand the current culture before embarking on a transformation effort. It is also very important to target both formal and informal leaders, provide mentoring and role modeling, offer incentives, select and retain appropriate personnel, employ problem-solving approaches, and engage stakeholders with diverse perspectives. Although empirical work on development and maintenance of subcultures is not substantial enough to warrant specific conclusions, we suggest that the Army be aware of the potential issue of subcultures when considering culture and climate change efforts.

Applying Approaches to the Army

Evidence-based prescriptions for how to change culture and climate are currently elusive. Rather, theoretical development outstrips available empirical evidence. Nonetheless, this is clearly a topic of great interest—organizational culture change is widely considered a necessity and a process that can be implemented. Certainly, Martins's (2011) review suggests that organizational change, especially when executed in a holistic fashion that includes a variety of interventions and intervention targets, can have a positive influence on desirable organizational outcomes, including productivity and employee job attitudes. Thus, organizational culture change can work. As would be expected, the drivers our literature review uncovered are similar in nature to drivers and prescriptions in the general change implementation literature (e.g., Burke, 2002, 2014; Fernandez and Rainey, 2006); we recommend employing a holistic approach, as does the literature, and concentrating on behaviors that are measurable and actionable. We also note that the literature from the sports industry (albeit limited to just six documents in our review, none of which used robust empirical designs), which is both masculine-dominated and team-oriented, may offer some lessons that are particularly relevant to the military. For example, Walker and Sartore-Baldwin (2013) found that men's college basketball is indeed hypermasculine, exclusive of women, and resistant to change. Accordingly, they suggest that leaders take organizational culture into account when developing policies to address gender inequality and promote inclusion of underrepresented groups. Additionally, the team-orientation approach taken by athletic coaches can be used to ingrain core values specific to the team and to recruit athletes who embrace those values relatively quickly to influence organizational culture change (Schroeder and Scribner, 2006).

Recommendations

We offer eight additional recommendations for developers of U.S. Army doctrine and policy interested in driving organizational culture change to address the Army's biggest challenges. These are presented on the basis of the synthesized findings. Note that these recommendations are roughly ordered temporally, but in implementation many of the recommendations activities would overlap—and all are important.

Define Organizational Culture

In attempting to change the organizational culture, a necessary first step is to define what organizational culture means. We recommend using Schein's (1990) definition[1] as a starting point because of its common use in the literature, clarity, emphasis on depth of culture, change-orientation, and use of both top-down and bottom-up perspectives.

Adopt a Common Definition of Army Organizational Culture

We suggest that the Army adopt a new definition of organizational culture that is both specific enough to fit with the Army domain and general enough to cover changes that occur within that domain. We would also recommend reevaluation of the definition of climate to reflect the consensus that it, too, involves shared perceptions of policies and practices and is not simply morale. While still very general, our definitional rec-

---

1 "Culture is a pattern of shared basic assumptions, invented, discovered, or developed by a given group as it learns to cope with its problems of external adaptation and internal integration that has worked well enough to be considered valid, and, therefore, is to be taught to new members of the group as the correct way to perceive, think, and feel in relation to those problems reframing."

ommendations would help bring the Army's definition more in line with the current literature. It should guide the Army to accomplish the following:

- Address both the deep and surface level to manifest culture both through values and ideologies
- Align policies with the practices, competencies, and perceptions of organizational members (align the climate)
- Use both a top-down and bottom-up approach, involving strategic and formalized processes as well as informal socialization processes
- Convey an openness to change to set the tone for continually adapting to change and transformation.

It is important to work from a common framework when developing a change intervention. In addition, adopting a definition with the characteristics outlined above can help ensure that relevant aspects are considered, particularly because different organizational levels may manifest culture somewhat differently (e.g., at some levels following orders exemplifies the value of duty, while at other levels members have the duty to challenge orders if they are incongruent with Army end goals). Surface-level artifacts or symbols can call attention to certain values, e.g., rewarding a servicemember for receiving treatment for a psychological health issue.

In addition, a deeper understanding of why things are done a certain way is important for understanding institutional change. In particular, the Army's main purpose is to defend the nation, and the historically rooted role of the warrior culture is a foundation for achieving this goal. It is important to acknowledge that policies cannot have their strongest effect without aligning them to a given goal; it is not sufficient to simply label something as a "core value" without aligning resources, competencies, and ultimately behavior patterns and perceptions of members in a definition.[2]

Further, the overall mission or strategy of the organization should be taken into that consideration. We also suggest selecting a definition of change that is both top-down and bottom-up because cultures generally involve both processes—strategic and formalized processes (that are especially relevant in the Army) along with naturally occurring selection and socialization of new members. Including a definition that emphasizes openness to change is also important because it sets the tone for continually adapting to change and transformation.

Lastly, tailoring the definition to the needs of the Army domain will best guide organizational change. Although we propose Schein's (1990) definition as a starting point, it should by no means be considered the end point.

---

[2] Note that although we are explicitly addressing the definitional issues surrounding culture, this alignment requirement by default takes into account aspects of an organization that tend to fall under definitions of "climate."

Determine Target Problems Amenable to Culture Change

We recommend that the Army first undertake organizational change within the context of a specific problem (Schein, 2010) and then understand the cultural implications of trying to solve that problem. In fact, we recommended that any attempt to undertake a change of the entire culture be avoided unless absolutely necessary. Given that organizational change is often a time- and other resource-consuming endeavor, the change effort should be focused. The Army, as noted, has a long and storied history, with established cultures and subcultures. It helps to set out the parameters of a specific problem, such as hostile workforce behavior, to delineate the necessary change and enable ways of thinking about how to change specific behaviors and underlying values and assumptions embodied in these behaviors. Further, cultural values or assumptions can be leveraged if they align with the desired changes. Although holism is key, as noted by Schein (2004) it is difficult to grasp the entirety of a culture before initiating a change effort. Also, engaging outsiders to an organization may help ease change, as they (in conjunction with insiders) may be able to highlight some of the less visible aspects of culture. The iceberg metaphor is commonly applied to discussions of culture, where only the tip is visible and much of the relevant content is underneath the surface.

Assess the Army's Current Culture and Climate in the Problem Context

We also recommend that the Army assess the current culture and climate to best determine how to address the most pressing problems and make that assessment within the focus on the target problem as just described. The Army is a huge organization with diverse missions, skill sets, and suborganizations. Leaders must prioritize those elements of culture that are relevant to the problem of interest and the goals being targeted. Assessing cultural perceptions across levels of analysis is a useful approach to identify possible subcultures within the larger organization (see González-Romá and Hernandez's discussion of climate uniformity, 2014) and manage those issues appropriately.

However, a holistic approach can be applied when using a specific problem set as a springboard and to help set parameters. This would entail considering various aspects of human resource management, such as training, incentives, and work design, as well as information and controlling systems; how these aspects align with respect to the problem at hand and their effects on culture and climate; and what messages changes in these aspects and systems would send.

Prioritize Organizational Culture Change

Our fifth recommendation is that senior Army leaders clearly articulate strategic goals to facilitate priority setting for competing initiatives or delegate that authority appropriately. This will help instill trust at all levels within the organization that appropriate actions will be supported. It is also necessary to allocate sufficient time, training, measurement and tracking capacity, and other more tangible resources to maximize successful change. The military today faces a number of strategic goals and mission demands. Mission command is critical to the success of organizations as they adapt to new strategic imperatives and changing operational demands. Unit leaders' prioritization efforts can help unit personnel distinguish what is mission critical, mission essential, and mission enhancing. Given that the work of the Army is to secure the nation, in some sense all missions are critical. However, a popular saying has it that if everything is urgent, nothing is in fact urgent. This observation points to the fact that priorities must be set to get important things done. Schein (2004) notes that culture arises from what leaders pay attention to—what they measure, what they reinforce, what they model, how they react to events. Therefore, part of leadership is choosing what to prioritize, and culture or climate change must be given the appropriate priority if the efforts are to succeed.

One perspective that emerged from this study is that the driving forces of institutional culture change in the Army that optimize human performance are mission critical. The Army must address how it is going to embrace institutional change, optimizing the human performance aspects of behavioral health, conduct in the workplace, changing demographics, and the use of new technologies to remain successful in the 21st century. A 20th-century Army perspective on institutional culture change that optimizes human performance seldom advanced beyond "mission enhancing" to "mission essential." As the Army continues to draw down its total force and must more intently assess its human capabilities, considerations of institutional change that optimize human performance and organizational growth become more than "mission enhancing" or "mission essential." They become, as this report suggests, "mission critical."

Develop a Strategy for Change with Clear Goals

We recommend that the Army develop a clear strategy and goals to guide change planning and implementation. This approach is consistent with Army culture; further, a change effort organized around clear goals and coupled with other individual behavior change efforts is more likely to be institutionalized and maintained. For example, as noted earlier, the Australian Army has seen notable cultural change as a result of its clear and unambiguous articulation of the "culture of intent" wholeheartedly supported by leadership at the top of the command chain. Emphasizing personal accountability and responsibility for the expected behavior and tracking progress toward behavior-based goals may make it possible for change to happen even before formal policy implementation, which can often take a long time to formulate and implement.

Engage Stakeholders at All Levels in the Army

We recommend that the Army engage all levels of leadership through the command chain and through noncommissioned officer support channels outside the chain of command to address both overarching goals and goals specific to different subcultures.

For example, obtaining input from those directly engaged in combat as well as from those responsible for strategy may provide multiple perspectives that all contribute to the overall goal(s). Within the Army culture, it is common to employ a top-down, hierarchical strategy for articulating a vision. This process generally starts by engaging senior leadership in communicating goals and planning strategy as well as inspiring institutional change. This vision is then stepped down through the chain of command to infiltrate subordinates with more specific goals, as they are pertinent to that level. At the same time, leadership must pay attention to local issues for successful implementation, particularly to address the specific goals of the different subcultures in such a large and diverse force. This may include engaging individuals outside of established chains of command (e.g., chaplains) but whose local influence may be strong. Full-scale institutionally coordinated efforts would certainly involve the U.S. Army Headquarters G-3/5/7 staff and the U.S. Army Training and Doctrine Command.

Consider Targeted Training to Maximize Resources and Uptake

Although training is a driver that is used heavily in the military, it may not be sufficient by itself to change organizational culture if processes are not in place to enable trainees to perform new skills (Schein, 2004). Thus, engaging peer and supervisor support is critical to guarantee training transfer. Transfer might be enabled by providing opportunities to practice new skills and otherwise integrating those new skills into routine processes (Brown and Sitzmann, 2011; Burke and Hutchins, 2007). We also recommend that training be targeted to subgroups (e.g., certain units) to maximize success. In addition to targeting both formal and informal leaders as critical change agents to influence institutional unit members (and the climates or shared perceptions in these units), it may be important to consider delivering some types of training in a targeted manner. Military servicemembers are inundated with all types of training, and the mere piling-on of more training activities is both burdensome and impractical. In the context of this discussion, it is important to highlight distinctions between mission-critical, mission-essential, and mission-enhancing Army training. Capabilities-based assessments can be structured to determine requirements for training, especially when Army doctrine and education do not fully address emerging or changing policy. Capabilities-based assessments can be used by an organization to recategorize mission-enhancing training as mission essential or mission critical (e.g., classes on drinking and driving or sexual harassment).

Too much training may lead to inattention and poor participation. Moreover, to ensure training transfers to the workplace, it is helpful to engage peer and supervisor support as well as otherwise aligning the workplace climate to enable that transfer. Therefore, it may be worthwhile to consider where to target training to get the most benefit with limited training and support resources. While it is optimal that the entire force be trained equivalently on all topics, competing mission-related training requirements as well as general training requirements make that approach infeasible, particularly if the training content is less relevant or is in response to rare or geographically concentrated events that are unlikely to persist over time. As an example of complexity, for highly specialized units in which women are not present, gender sensitivity training may have little immediate benefit. However, it may also be those units that most need the training because of limited exposure. Timing the training such that the lessons could be "practiced" during interaction with women would be more likely to change behavior and thus would be more valuable in such situations. On the other hand, training soldiers about coping with behavioral health problems may be of broader benefit not only for personal resilience (Meredith et al., 2011) but also for increasing awareness of others in the unit and knowing the signs of risk and when to step in and help.

Conclusion

A number of challenges are currently confronting the U.S. Army, including adverse consequences of combat and repeated deployments; perceived stigma associated with mental health care seeking; and sexual harassment and assault in the workplace. A clearly defined and elucidated understanding of Army organizational culture among servicemembers, commanders, and senior leaders is key to adaptation to the many changes taking place. Our study reached the following conclusions:

- The literature review identified over 80 definitions of organizational culture potentially applicable to the Army. To be aligned with the Army, an updated definition should cover depth, openness to change, and allow for both top-down and bottom-up change processes.
- Review of the literature found five top drivers of organizational culture change:
  - Goals: setting clear goals; using coherent planning, persistence, and strategic thinking; results oriented
  - Accountability: sharing responsibility and accountability
  - Training: developing personnel through training (i.e., skills, engagement, education, etc.)
  - Resources: devoting sufficient resources (i.e., financial, staffing, time, etc.) to change efforts
  - Stakeholders: engaging both formal and informal leaders.

- SMEs identified four actions that may be taken as a first step in affecting culture and climate change:
  - Define the problem.
  - Understand current culture.
  - Define/articulate the desired culture or vision.
  - Identify specific goals.

Changing culture is difficult across an organization because it is also necessary to change individual values, beliefs, attitudes, and behaviors within the organization. Nevertheless, change is possible in the Army, particularly through the use of a holistic approach that focuses drivers of change in a coordinated manner. Change is also more likely if problems to be solved are clearly specified and articulated. Finally, despite the inherent hierarchical structure of the Army, engaging people at all levels of the organization will facilitate organizational change, as leadership responsibility is present at every level.

APPENDIX A

Additional Details About the Literature Review

This appendix provides information about each of the elements coded or abstracted from the 549 documents we coded from the literature review. For each of the coding categories, we included operational definitions and explanations for the different codes.

Category	Coding Options	Operational Definition(s)
Exclude		Should the article be excluded based on the following criteria:
	International	Article is about countries besides the United States. This includes comparative articles (i.e., those that compare U.S. organizations to non–U.S. organizations).
	Not relevant	Article does not have to do with organizational culture/climate.
	Not culture	Article is only tangentially related to culture/climate or culture/climate is a secondary part of the article.
Document type		What category of published work does this document fall under?
	Experimental	Empirical study with causal design (experimenter-controlled conditions and random assignment).
	Quasi-experimental	Empirical study with causal design (experimenter-controlled conditions but not random assignment).
	Longitudinal	Empirical study with repeated assessments but without causal design (no experimenter-controlled conditions/random assignment).
	Observational	Empirical study without causal design (no experimenter-controlled conditions/random assignment).
	Review	Synthesis of a literature.
	Policy report/directive	Reviews policy or offers recommendations.
	Other (specify):	
Document type (specify)		For empirical documents, what was the study design? For nonempirical documents, what was done?
Method		What methods were used to answer the research question? (more precise than document type)

Category	Coding Options	Operational Definition(s)
	Quantitative	Included standard measures with assigned numeric values; descriptive and inferential statistics.
	Qualitative	Included descriptive measures; maybe some descriptive statistics.
	Mixed methods	Combination of both.
	Not applicable	
Data collection method		What data collection methods did the document use?
	Expert panel/ focus group	Subject matter experts were consulted, for purposes of establishing feasibility, validity, etc.; OR asked a group of people questions about their knowledge, experiences, beliefs, attitudes on a particular topic in an interactive setting; online or in-person.
	Interview	Structured or unstructured; conducted over phone, online, or in-person.
	Survey/ questionnaire	Included a group of standardized scales, subscales, or items; filled out over phone, online, or in-person.
	Observational coding	Researchers systematically observed and coded participants' behavior.
	Secondary analysis/ document review	Reviews data from secondary sources, such as archival datasets, documents/records, archives.
	Not applicable	
Relevant unit of analysis		What unit of analysis did the document focus on?
	National	Organizational data was collected/analyzed at the country level; includes multiple organizations.
	Region	Organizational data from a section (or multiple sections) within a country; includes more than one state, and multiple organizations.
	State	Organizational data at the state level; includes multiple organizations and looks at state differences.
	Organization	Compares data on one or more organizations.
	Unit/team	Organizational data on subunit(s) or team(s) within an organization.
	Individual	Organizational data collected from individuals within a unit or organization that can't be statistically aggregated or generalized beyond the individual.
	Other (specify)	
	Not applicable	
# Unit(s) (specify)		Describe the populations within all applicable units of analysis (i.e., unit labels and, if available, numbers within each).

Category	Coding Options	Operational Definition(s)
Industry		What industry does the document examine?
	Military	Includes any/all branches of the U.S. military.
	First responders	Industries involved in emergency response (not related to health care).
	Health/medical	Industries directly involved in medicine, healthcare delivery, and treatment.
	Professional sports	Industries that recruit, train, and manage professional athletes/ teams.
	Corporate	For-profit business entities.
	Other (specify)	If other, document is EXCLUDED, specify the industry and move on to the next article for extraction.
Climate	X or blank	Does the document self-identify as a "climate" piece?
Specificity		How general or specific is the document's perspective on culture/ climate?
	General	Refers to a general climate or culture, and/or its valence (i.e., good or bad; positive or negative), but doesn't specify a domain.
	Domain-specific	Refers to a particular domain of culture/climate (e.g., safety, diversity, service, respect, innovation, etc.). Should be explicit!
Subculture(s)		What type of subculture(s) is discussed—if applicable?
	Orthogonal	Applies to subculture(s) that uphold the core values of the dominant culture, but also have unique, nonconflicting ones.
	Enhancing	Applies to subculture(s) with even stronger adherence to core values of the dominant culture than others.
	Counter	Applies to subculture(s) directly challenging the core values of the dominant culture.
	Ambiguous	A subculture(s) was mentioned, but not enough detail to assign a category.
	Not applicable	No subculture(s) mentioned.
Subculture(s) (describe)		The document's verbatim description of the subculture(s) (copy/ paste and provide page # if applicable).
Target content one–four		The "what" of culture or climate; the focal content the document is targeting or trying to change.
	Values/attitudes/ beliefs	Targets (perceptions of) an organization's core priorities or assumptions; also includes communication of these priorities (by leadership or org members).
	Norms	Targets (perceptions of) the shared expectations for ways to think and behave; Includes attraction-selection-attrition and other socialization processes for promoting behaviors that are in line with organizational values, and discouraging those that conflict.

Category	Coding Options	Operational Definition(s)
	Symbols	Targets (perceptions of) an organization's physical objects/ structural artifacts that are given meaning and reinforce a shared identity or underlying values.
	Knowledge/ skills/resources	Targets (perceptions of) an organization's practices for providing information, skills, and resources (financial, technological, etc.).
Target mechanism (select one)		The "how" of culture or climate; What the document describes as the major mechanism or action lever for the desired culture/ climate. (Select one that most applies).
	Selection	Document emphasizes attracting, selecting, and/or retaining organizational members and leaders in line with the espoused culture or climate; person-organization fit is viewed as the action lever.
	Training/ mentoring	Document emphasizes training members and/or support of continued learning and career development.
	Monitoring/ control	Document emphasizes planning; measuring/tracking progress toward goals or outcomes.
	Not applicable	
Outcome(s)		What is the ultimate (desired) consequence of the culture/climate?
	Financial	Outcomes pertaining to the cost-efficiency or competitive financial performance of the organization.
	Behavioral	Outcomes pertaining to observable actions on the part of organizational members. Can also refer to putting a stop to some action.
	Social	Outcomes pertaining to the social interactions among organizational members, and other team/group-related outcomes, as well as perceptions of these interactions/group factors.
	Psychological	Outcomes pertaining to the emotions, beliefs/attitudes, and perceptions of organizational members.
	Other (specify)	
	Not applicable	No organizational outcome was discussed.
Outcome(s) (specify)		Specify the target outcomes.
Policy recommendations		What policy recommendations for org culture or climate does the document provide—if applicable? Or, what are the take-away points of potential interest to stakeholders?
Definition		How does the document operationalize culture or climate? (Cite original sources of these definitions, if included.)
Drivers		What factors may promote, hinder, or otherwise control the culture or climate (or culture/climate change)? List content of interventions if applicable.

Documents Included in Literature Review

1. Aarons, Gregory. A., and Angelina. C. Sawitzky, "Organizational Culture and Climate and Mental Health Provider Attitudes Toward Evidence-Based Practice," *Psychological Services*, Vol. 3, No. 1, February 2006, pp. 61–72.
2. Aboud, Antone, "Incident Management, Organizational Culture, and Honest Communications," *Mental Retardation*, Vol. 44, No. 6, December 2006, pp. 438–442.
3. Adams, Gordon , Neyla Arnas, Charles Barry, William I. Bacchus, Hans Binnendijk, R. Stephen Brent, Bernard Carreau, Patrick M. Cronin, Leslie B. Curtin, Christel Fonzo-Eberhard, David Glaudemans, L. Erik Kjonnerod, Richard L. Kugler, Christopher J. Lamb, Bernd "Bear" McConnell, Terry J. Pudas, James A. Schear, Kristine Shelstad, Catherine Theohary, Linton Wells, Larry Wentz, and John W. Yaeger, *Civilian Surge. Key to Complex Operations*, Washington, D.C.: National Defense University, 2008.
4. Adrian, Nicole, "A LEAN Transformation," *Quality Progress*, Vol. 44, No. 2, 2011, pp. 40–45.
5. Ainsworth, Frank, and Leon C. Fulcher, "Creating and Sustaining a Culture of Group Care," *Child & Youth Services*, Vol. 28, No. 1–2, 2006, pp. 151–176.
6. Alberta, Anthony J., Richard R. Ploski, and Scott L. Carlson, "Addressing Challenges to Providing Peer-Based Recovery Support," *Journal of Behavioral Health Services and Research*, Vol. 39, No. 4, October 2012, pp. 481–491.
7. Alidina, Shenaz, Meredith B. Rosenthal, Eric C. Schneider, Sara J. Singer, and Mark W. Friedberg, "Practice Environments and Job Satisfaction in Patient-Centered Medical Homes," *Annals of Family Medicine*, Vol. 12, No. 4, July 2014, pp. 331–337.
8. Allen, Nicole E., Amy Lehrner, Erica Mattison, Teresa Miles, and Angela Russell, "Promoting Systems Change in the Health Care Response to Domestic Violence," *Journal of Community Psychology*, Vol. 35, No. 1, January 2007, pp. 103–120.
9. Allen, Scott J., "A Hunt for the Missing 50 Cents: One Piece of the Leadership Development Puzzle," *Organization Development Journal*, Vol. 26, No. 1, 2008, pp. 19–29.

10. Anderson, Dean, "An Integrated System for Organizational Transformation," *Journal of Integral Theory and Practice*, Vol. 8, No. 1–2, June 2013, pp. 1–18.
11. Appelbaum, Steven, Kyle J. Deguire, and Mathieu Lay, "The Relationship of Ethical Climate to Deviant Workplace Behaviour," *Corporate Governance: The International Journal of Effective Board Performance*, Vol. 5, No. 4, 2005, pp. 43–55.
12. Appelbaum, Steven H., Giulio David Iaconi, and Albert Matousek, "Positive and Negative Deviant Workplace Behaviors: Causes, Impacts, and Solutions," *Corporate Governance: The International Journal of Effective Board Performance*, Vol. 7, No. 5, 2007, pp. 586–598.
13. Appelbaum, Steven H., and Barbara T. Shapiro, "Diagnosis and Remedies for Deviant Workplace Behaviors," *Journal of American Academy of Business, Cambridge*, Vol. 9, No. 2, September, 2006, p. 14.
14. Ardichvili, Alexandre, "Sustainability or Limitless Expansion: Paradigm Shift in HRD Practice and Teaching," *European Journal of Training & Development*, Vol. 36, No. 9, 2012, pp. 873–887.
15. Armenakis, Achilles, Steven Brown, and Anju Mehta, "Organizational Culture: Assessment and Transformation," *Journal of Change Management*, Vol. 11, No. 3, 2011, pp. 305–328.
16. Armenakis, Achilles, and Irene Lang, "Forensic Diagnosis and Transformation of an Organizational Culture," *Journal of Change Management*, Vol. 14, No. 2, 2014, pp. 149–170.
17. Armenakis, Achilles, and Jeffrey Wigand, "Stakeholder Actions and Their Impact on the Organizational Cultures of Two Tobacco Companies," *Business & Society Review*, Vol. 115, No. 2, Summer 2010, pp. 147–171.
18. Arnetz, Judith E., Ludmila S. Zhdanova, Dalia Elsouhag, Peter Lichtenberg, Mark R. Luborsky, and Bengt B. Arnetz, "Organizational Climate Determinants of Resident Safety Culture in Nursing Homes," *Gerontologist*, Vol. 51, No. 6, December 2011, pp. 739–749.
19. Arriaza, Gilberto, "Changing Schools for Good: A Study of School Culture and Systems," *Education and Society*, Vol. 22, No. 2, 2004, pp. 5–21.
20. Austin, Manila, and Debra A. Harkins, "Assessing Change: Can Organizational Learning 'Work' for Schools?" Learning Organization, Vol. 15, No. 2, 2008, pp. 105–125.
21. Ayers, David F., "Developing Climates for Renewal in the Community College: A Case Study of Dissipative Self-Organization," *Community College Journal of Research and Practice*, Vol. 26, No. 2, 2002, pp. 165–185.
22. ———, "Organizational Climate in Its Semiotic Aspect: A Postmodern Community College Undergoes Renewal," *Community College Review*, Vol. 33, No. 1, Fall 2005, pp. 1–21.

23. Baird, Lynn N., "ALOHA to New Learning: Uniting Student and Career Staff Through Training," *Journal of Access Services*, Vol. 5, No. 1–2, 2007, pp. 121–132.
24. Baker, G. Ross, Hannah King, Jeanne L. MacDonald, and Jeffrey D. Horbar, "Using Organizational Assessment Surveys for Improvement in Neonatal Intensive Care," *Pediatrics*, Vol. 111, No. 4, Part 2, April 2003, pp. e419–e425.
25. Balling, Rolf, "Diagnosis of Organizational Cultures," *Transactional Analysis Journal*, Vol. 35, No. 4, October, 2005, pp. 313–320.
26. Banaszak-Holl, Jane, Nicholas G. Castle, Michael Lin, and Gretchen Spreitzer, "An Assessment of Cultural Values and Resident-Centered Culture Change in U.S. Nursing Facilities," *Health Care Management Review*, Vol. 38, No. 4, October–December 2013, pp. 295–305.
27. Banutu-Gomez, Michael, and Shandra M. T. Banutu-Gomez, "Leadership and Organizational Change in a Competitive Environment," *Business Renaissance Quarterly*, Vol. 2, No. 2, Summer 2007, p. 69.
28. Barriere, Michael T., Betty R. Anson, Robin S. Ording, and Evelyn Rogers, "Culture Transformation in a Health Care Organization: A Process for Building Adaptive Capabilities Through Leadership Development," *Consulting Psychology Journal: Practice and Research*, Vol. 54, No. 2, 2002, pp. 116–130.
29. Baumann, Barbara L., David J. Kolko, Kathryn Collins, and Amy D. Herschell, "Understanding Practitioners' Characteristics and Perspectives Prior to the Dissemination of an Evidence-Based Intervention," *Child Abuse & Neglect*, Vol. 30, No. 7, July 2006, pp. 771–787.
30. Baumgartner, Rupert J., and Christian Zielowski, "Analyzing Zero Emission Strategies Regarding Impact on Organizational Culture and Contribution to Sustainable Development," *Journal of Cleaner Production*, Vol. 15, No. 13–14, 2007, pp. 1321–1327.
31. Bea, J. R., "Focus on Culture," *Health Forum Journal*, Vol. 45, No. 4, July–August 2002, p. 6.
32. Beaver, Graham, "Editorial: Adapting Culture to Embrace Creativity and Innovation," *Strategic Change*, Vol. 13, No. 7, December 2004, pp. 343–344.
33. Belassi, Walid, Alex Z. Kondra, and Oya Icmeli Tukel, "New Product Development Projects: The Effects of Organizational Culture," *Project Management Journal*, Vol. 38, No. 4, December 2007, pp. 12–24.
34. Bell, Myrtle P., James C. Quick, and Cynthia S. Cycyota, "Assessment and Prevention of Sexual Harassment of Employees: An Applied Guide to Creating Healthy Organizations," *International Journal of Selection and Assessment*, Vol. 10, No. 1–2, March–June 2002, pp. 160–167.
35. Bell, R. Greg, K. Matthew Gilley, and John Médaille, "Ethics and Institutions: Taking a Closer Look at Rewards," *Journal of Business Ethics Education*, Vol. 10, 2013, pp. 261–274.

36. Bell, Simon J., Bülent Mengüc, and Robert E. Widing II, "Salesperson Learning, Organizational Learning, and Retail Store Performance," *Journal of the Academy of Marketing Science*, Vol. 38, No. 2, April 2010, pp. 187–201.
37. Bellot, Jennifer, "Defining and Assessing Organizational Culture," *Nursing Forum*, Vol. 46, No. 1, January–March 2011, pp. 29–37.
38. ———, "Nursing Home Culture Change: What Does It Mean to Nurses?" *Research in Gerontology Nursing*, Vol. 5, No. 4, October 2012, pp. 264–273.
39. Benjamin, Bret, Tripti Gulliya, and Alexander W. Crispo, "Emotional Intelligence and Organizational Culture," *Insights to a Changing World Journal*, No. 1, 2012, p. 52.
40. Berlowitz, Dan R., Gary J. Young, Elaine C. Hickey, Debra Saliba, Brian S. Mittman, Elaine Czarnowski, Barbara Simon, Jennifer J. Anderson, Arlene S. Ash, Lisa V. Rubenstein, and Mark A. Moskowitz, "Quality Improvement Implementation in the Nursing Home," *Health Services Research*, Vol. 38, No. 1, Part 1, February 2003, pp. 65–83.
41. Berry, Benisa, "Organizational Culture: A Framework and Strategies for Facilitating Employee Whistleblowing," *Employee Responsibilities and Rights Journal*, Vol. 16, No. 1, March 2004, pp. 1–11.
42. Bickerstaff, David A., "Changing Interagency Culture," *Lucent*, pp. 20–28.
43. Boan, David M., "Cognitive-Behavior Modification and Organizational Culture," *Consulting Psychology Journal: Practice and Research*, Vol. 58, No. 1, 2006, pp. 51–61.
44. Boden, Daniel, Maura Borrego, and Lynita K. Newswander, "Student Socialization in Interdisciplinary Doctoral Education," *Higher Education*, Vol. 62, No. 6, December 2011, pp. 741–755.
45. Bograd, Sandra, "Outbehaving the Competition," *Contract Management*, October 2009, pp. 52–57.
46. Bohmer, Richard M. J., Jonathan D. Bloom, Elizabeth A. Mort, Akinluwa A. Demehin, and Gregg S. Meyer, "Restructuring Within an Academic Health Center to Support Quality and Safety: The Development of the Center for Quality and Safety at the Massachusetts General Hospital," *Academic Medicine*, Vol. 84, No. 12, December 2009, pp. 1663–1671.
47. Bolton, Patrick, Markus K. Brunnermeier, and Laura Veldkamp, "Leadership, Coordination, and Corporate Culture," *Review of Economic Studies*, Vol. 80, No. 2, April 2013, pp. 512–537.
48. Bond, Meg A., and Michelle C. Haynes, "Workplace Diversity: A Social-Ecological Framework and Policy Implications," *Social Issues and Policy Review*, Vol. 8, No. 1, January 2014, pp. 167–201.
49. Boss, R. Wayne, Benjamin B. Dunford, Alan D. Boss, and Mark L. McConkie, "Sustainable Change in the Public Sector: The Longitudinal Benefits of Orga-

nization Development," *Journal of Applied Behavioral Science*, Vol. 46, No. 4, December 2010, pp. 436–472.

50. Boutros, Akram, "How to Make Innovation Happen—Part 3," *Physician Executive*, Vol. 33, No. 4, July–August 2007, pp. 56–59.
51. Bowen, David E., and Cheri Ostroff, "Understanding HRM-Firm Performance Linkages: The Role of the 'Strength' of the HRM System," *Academy of Management Review*, Vol. 29, No. 2, April 2004, pp. 203–221.
52. Bradley, Elizabeth H., Ingrid M. Nembhard, Christina T. Yuan, Amy F. Stern, Jeptha P. Curtis, Brahmajee K. Nallamothu, John Brush, Jr., and Harlan M. Krumholz, "What Is the Experience of National Quality Campaigns? Views from the Field," *Health Services Research*, Vol. 45, No. 6, Part 1, December 2010, pp. 1651–1669.
53. Brady, William H., and Shar Haley, "Storytelling Defines Your Organizational Culture," *Physician Executive*, Vol. 39, No. 1, January–February 2013, pp. 40–43.
54. Brannen, Donald E., Mark A. McDonnell, and Amy Schmitt, "Organizational Culture on Community Health Outcomes After the 2009 H1N1 Pandemic," *Journal of Organizational Culture, Communications and Conflict*, Vol. 17, No. 1, January 2013, pp. 1–18.
55. Briggs, Elten, Fernando Jaramillo, and William A. Weeks, "The Influences of Ethical Climate and Organization Identity Comparisons on Salespeople and Their Job Performance," *Journal of Personal Selling & Sales Management*, Vol. 32, No. 4, 2012, pp. 421–436.
56. Briody, Elizabeth, Tracy M. Pester, and Robert Trotter, "A Story's Impact on Organizational-Culture Change," *Journal of Organizational Change Management*, Vol. 25, No. 1, 2012, pp. 67–87.
57. Brown, Mark S., Judy Ohlinger, Connie Rusk, Paula Delmore, Patricia Ittmann, and Care Group, "Implementing Potentially Better Practices for Multidisciplinary Team Building: Creating a Neonatal Intensive Care Unit Culture of Collaboration," *Pediatrics*, Vol. 111, No. 4, Part 2, April 2003, pp. e482–e488.
58. Brownell, Judi, "Applied Research in Managerial Communication: The Critical Link Between Knowledge and Practice," *Cornell Hotel and Restaurant Administration Quarterly*, Vol. 44, April, 2003, pp. 39–49.
59. Browning, Blair W., and Suzanne E. Boys, "Extending the Conversation: Examining Culture Change Through the Lens of Interim Leadership," *OD Practitioner*, Vol. 44, No. 1, 2012, pp. 18–23.
60. Bruhn, John G., "Managing Tough and Easy Organizational Cultures," *Health Care Manager (Frederick)*, Vol. 20, No. 2, December 2001, pp. 1–10.
61. Bruhn, John G., and Josiah Lowrey, "The Good and Bad About Greed: How the Manifestations of Greed Can Be Used to Improve Organizational and Indi-

vidual Behavior and Performance," *Consulting Psychology Journal: Practice and Research*, Vol. 64, No. 2, June 2012, pp. 136–150.

62. Buch, Kimberly, and David K. Wetzel, "Analyzing and Realigning Organizational Culture," *Leadership & Organization Development Journal*, Vol. 22, No. 1, 2001, pp. 40–44.
63. Bucher, Jacob, "General issue (G.I.) Strain: Applying Strain Theory to Military Offending," *Deviant Behavior*, Vol. 32, No. 9, 2011, pp. 846–875.
64. Buckley, Peter F., and Robert K. Grigsby, "A Propitious Moment in the Midst of Crisis: A Case Study of Organizational Change in an Academic Department," *Academic Psychiatry*, Vol. 35, No. 2, March–April 2011, pp. 143–148.
65. Bumstead, Alaina, and Thomas E. Boyce, "Exploring the Effects of Cultural Variables in the Implementation of Behavior-Based Safety in Two Organizations," *Journal of Organizational Behavior Management*, Vol. 24, No. 4, 2004, pp. 43–63.
66. Buono, Anthony F., and Kenneth W. Kerber, "The Challenge of Organizational Change: Enhancing Organizational Change Capacity," *Revue Sciences de Gestion*, Vol. 65, 2008, pp. 99–118.
67. Burke, W. Warner, "A Perspective on the Field of Organization Development and Change: The Zeigarnik Effect," *Journal of Applied Behavioral Science*, Vol. 47, No. 2, June 2011, pp. 143–167.
68. ———, "Organizational Change," in Schneider, Benjamin and Karen M. Barbera, eds., *The Oxford Handbook of Organizational Climate and Culture*, New York: Oxford University Press, 2014.
69. Burrell, Darrell Norman, "Why Small Private Liberal Arts Colleges Need to Develop Effective Marketing Cultures," *Journal of Strategic Marketing*, Vol. 16, No. 3, 2008, pp. 267–278.
70. Bushardt, Stephen C., David W. Glascoff, and D. Harold Doty, "Organizational Culture, Formal Reward Structure, and Effective Strategy Implementation: A Conceptual Model," *Journal of Organizational Culture, Communications and Conflict*, Vol. 15, No. 2, July 2011, pp. 57–70.
71. Bushardt, Stephen C., John Lambert, and David L. Duhon, "Selecting a Better Carrot: Organizational Learning, Formal Rewards and Culture—A Behavioral Perspective," *Journal of Organizational Culture, Communications and Conflict*, Vol. 11, No. 2, July 2007, pp. 67–79.
72. Busse, Ronald, "Corporate Culture, Organizational Change and Meaning at Work—Linking Human Resources with Business Ethics," *Human Systems Management*, Vol. 33, No. 1–2, 2014, pp. 47–50.
73. Campbell, Constance, "A Longitudinal Study of One Organization's Culture: Do Values Endure?" *American Journal of Business*, Vol. 19, No. 2, 2004, pp. 41–52.

74. Campbell, Robert J., "Creating a Winning Organizational Culture," *Health Care Manager (Frederick)*, Vol. 28, No. 4, October–December 2009, pp. 328–343.
75. Carter, Danon, and Timothy Baghurst, "The Influence of Servant Leadership on Restaurant Employee Engagement," *Journal of Business Ethics*, Vol. 124, No. 3, October 2013, pp. 453–464.
76. Casida, Jesus, "Linking Nursing Unit's Culture to Organizational Effectiveness: A Measurement Tool," *Nursing Economic$*, Vol. 26, No. 2, March–April 2008, pp. 106–110.
77. Casida, Jesus, and Genevieve Pinto-Zipp, "Leadership-Organizational Culture Relationship in Nursing Units of Acute Care Hospitals," *Nursing Economic$*, Vol. 26, No. 1, January–February 2008, pp. 7–15.
78. Castle, Nicholas G., Steven Handler, John Engberg, and Kristen Sonon, "Nursing Home Administrators' Opinions of the Resident Safety Culture in Nursing Homes," *Health Care Management Review*, Vol. 32, No. 1, January–March 2007, pp. 66–76.
79. Chance, Sarah, Daren Dickson, Patricia Marrone Bennett, and Susan Stone, "Unlocking the Doors: How Fundamental Changes in Residential Care Can Improve the Ways We Help Children and Families," *Residential Treatment for Children & Youth*, Vol. 27, No. 2, 2010, pp. 127–148.
80. Chang, Evelyn T., Danielle E. Rose, Elizabeth M. Yano, Kenneth B. Wells, Maureen E. Metzger, Edward P. Post, Martin L. Lee, and Lisa V. Rubenstein, "Determinants of Readiness for Primary Care-Mental Health Integration (PC-MHI) in the VA Health Care System," *Journal of General Internal Medicine*, Vol. 28, No. 3, March 2013, pp. 353–362.
81. Cherry, Robert A., Deborah C. Davis, and Luanne Thorndyke, "Transforming Culture Through Physician Leadership Development," *Physician Executive*, Vol. 36, No. 3, May–June 2010, pp. 38–44.
82. Chinowsky, Paul, Keith Molenaar, and Allison Realph, "Learning Organizations in Construction," *Journal of Management in Engineering*, Vol. 23, No. 1, January 2007, pp. 27–34.
83. Choi, Myungweon, and Wendy E. A. Ruona, "Individual Readiness for Organizational Change and Its Implications for Human Resource and Organization Development," *Human Resource Development Review*, Vol. 10, No. 1, March 2011, pp. 46–73.
84. Christensen, Libby, "US Army Pacific Knowledge Management," *Army Communicator*, Vol. 27, No. 1, Spring 2002, pp. 6–8.
85. Chrobot-Mason, D., and N. P. Aramovich, "The Psychological Benefits of Creating an Affirming Climate for Workplace Diversity," *Group & Organization Management*, Vol. 38, No. 6, December 2013, pp. 659–689.

86. Chu, Carolyn, Brandon T. Dues, and Laura L. Miller, *Cultural Themes in Messages from Top Air Force Leaders, 2005–2008*, Santa Monica, Calif.: RAND Corporation, DB-583-AF, 2010.
87. Ciampa, Dan, and George Stalk, "Changing Your Company's Strategy? Better Change Its Personality, Too: The CEO-HR Executive Partnership," *People & Strategy*, Vol. 31, No. 2, April 2008, p. 22.
88. Clark, Cynthia M., Marcia Belcheir, Pamela Strohfus, and Pamela J. Springer, "Development and Description of the Culture/Climate Assessment Scale," *Journal of Nursing Education*, Vol. 51, No. 2, February 2012, pp. 75–80.
89. Clark, Olga L., Michael J. Zickar, and Steve M. Jex, "Role Definition as a Moderator of the Relationship Between Safety Climate and Organizational Citizenship Behavior Among Hospital Nurses," *Journal of Business and Psychology*, Vol. 29, No. 1, March 2014, pp. 101–110.
90. Clarke, Sharon, "The Contemporary Workforce: Implications for Organisational Safety Culture," *Personnel Review*, Vol. 32, No. 1–2, 2003, pp. 40–57.
91. Claxton, Chuck, "Placing Our Assumptions at Risk: Pathway to Changing the Culture of the Community College," *Community College Journal of Research and Practice*, Vol. 31, No. 3, 2007, pp. 217–229.
92. Cochran-Smith, Marilyn, and Boston College Evidence Team, "'Re-Culturing' Teacher Education: Inquiry, Evidence, and Action," *Journal of Teacher Education*, Vol. 60, No. 5, November/December 2009, pp. 458–468.
93. Cocowitch, Vic, Stephen Orton, Jacque Daniels, and Debbie Kiser, "Reframing Leadership Development in Healthcare: An OD Approach," *OD Practitioner*, Vol. 45, No. 3, 2013, pp. 10–18.
94. Cohen, Raphael S., "A Tale of Two Manuals," *Prism*, Vol. 2, No. 1, December 2010, pp. 87–100.
95. Collins, Frank, "Career Self-Interest and Concern for Others: The Effects of Co-Worker Attitudes on Fraudulent Behavior," *Accounting and the Public Interest*, Vol. 6, No. 1, December 2006, pp. 95–115.
96. Collins-Camargo, Crystal, and Kenneth Millar, "The Potential for a More Clinical Approach to Child Welfare Supervision to Promote Practice and Case Outcomes: A Qualitative Study in Four States," *The Clinical Supervisor*, Vol. 29, No. 2, 2010, pp. 164–187.
97. Conbere, John, and Alla Heorhiadi, "Preparing Physicians to Manage Conflict, or, How the Physician Leadership College Teaches Physicians to Use Interest-Based Processes," *Hamline Journal of Public Law and Policy*, Vol. 29, No. 2, Summer, 2008, pp. 261–268.
98. Conceição, Simone C.O., and Brian A. Altman, "Training and Development Process and Organizational Culture Change," *Organization Development Journal*, Vol. 29, No. 1, Spring 2011, pp. 33–43.

99. Condrey, Stephen E., Rex L. Facer, and John A. Hamilton, "Employees Amidst Welfare Reform: TANF Employees' Overall Job- and Organizational-Role Satisfaction," *Journal of Human Behavior in the Social Environment*, Vol. 12, No. 2–3, 2005, pp. 221–242.
100. Coomer, Karen, "Corporate Cultures," *Occupational Health*, Vol. 59, No. 4, April 2007, pp. 28–30.
101. Copley, Donald D., "Culture Change in Recruiting," *Army Sustainment*, Vol. 41, No. 5, September–October 2009, pp. 15–18.
102. Corazzini, Kirsten, "The Importance of Organizational Climate to Training Needs and Outcomes in Long-Term Care," *Alzheimer's Care Today*, Vol. 11, No. 2, April–June 2010, pp. 109–121.
103. Corley, Kevin G., "Defined by Our Strategy or Our Culture? Hierarchical Differences in Perceptions of Organizational Identity and Change," *Human Relations*, Vol. 57, No. 9, September 2004, pp. 1145–1177.
104. Corrigan, Patrick W., Sarah Diwan, John Campion, and Fadwa Rashid, "Transformational Leadership and the Mental Health Team," *Administration and Policy in Mental Health*, Vol. 30, No. 2, November 2002, pp. 97–108.
105. Corrigan, Patrick W., Sarah L. Diwan, Stanley G. McCracken, Kelvin Oliver, Annette Backs, Fadwa Rashid, John Campion, and Ruth Davies Farmer, "Organisational Correlates to Staff Attitudes About Behavioural Programs," *Behaviour Change*, Vol. 18, No. 2, 2001, pp. 114–123.
106. Cottingham, Ann, Anthony L. Suchman, Debra K. Litzelman, Richard M. Frankel, David L. Mossbarger, Penelope R. Williamson, DeWitt C. Baldwin, Jr., and Thomas S. Inui, "Erratum to: Enhancing the Informal Curriculum of a Medical School: A Case Study in Organizational Culture Change," *JGIM: Journal of General Internal Medicine*, Vol. 26, No. 3, 2011, p. 352.
107. Cottingham, Ann H., Anthony L. Suchman, Debra K. Litzelman, Richard M. Frankel, David L. Mossbarger, Penelope R. Williamson, DeWitt C. Baldwin, Jr., and Thomas S. Inui, "Enhancing the Informal Curriculum of a Medical School: A Case Study in Organizational Culture Change," *Journal of General Internal Medicine*, Vol. 23, No. 6, June 2008, pp. 715–722.
108. Courtney, Katherine O., George W. Joe, Grace A. Rowan-Szal, and D. Dwayne Simpson, "Using Organizational Assessment as a Tool for Program Change," *Journal of Substance Abuse Treatment*, Vol. 33, No. 2, September 2007, pp. 131–137.
109. Coustasse, Alberto, Douglas A. Mains, Kristine Lykens, Sue G. Lurie, and Fernando Trevino, "Organizational Culture in a Terminally Ill Hospital," *Journal of Hospital Marketing and Public Relations*, Vol. 18, No. 1, 2008, pp. 39–60.
110. Craigie, Frederic C., Jr., and Richard F. Hobbs III, "Exploring the Organizational Culture of Exemplary Community Health Center Practices," *Family Medicine Journal*, Vol. 36, No. 10, November–December 2004, pp. 733–738.

111. Crain, A. Lauren, Brian C. Martinson, and Carol R. Thrush, "Relationships Between the Survey of Organizational Research Climate (SORC) and Self-Reported Research Practices," *Science and Engineering Ethics*, Vol. 19, No. 3, September 2013, pp. 835–850.
112. Cretin, Shan, Donna O. Farley, Kathryn J. Dolter, and Will Nicholas, "Evaluating an Integrated Approach to Clinical Quality Improvement: Clinical Guidelines, Quality Measurement, and Supportive System Design," *Medical Care*, Vol. 39, No. 8, Supp. 2, August 2001, pp. II70–II84.
113. Crimmins, Timothy J., and Julia Halberg, "Measuring Success in Creating a 'Culture of Health,'" *Journal of Occupational and Environmental Medicine*, Vol. 51, No. 3, March 2009, pp. 351–355.
114. Curry, Leslie A., Erica Spatz, Emily Cherlin, Jennifer W. Thompson, David Berg, Henry H. Ting, Carole Decker, Harlan M. Krumholz, and Elizabeth H. Bradley, "What Distinguishes Top-Performing Hospitals in Acute Myocardial Infarction Mortality Rates?" *Annals of Internal Medicine*, Vol. 154, No. 6, 2011, pp. 384–390.
115. Dasborough, Marie T., Neal M. Ashkanasy, Eugene Y. J. Tee, and Herman H. M. Tse, "What Goes Around Comes Around: How Meso-Level Negative Emotional Contagion Can Ultimately Determine Organizational Attitudes Toward Leaders," *Leadership Quarterly*, Vol. 20, No. 4, August 2009, pp. 571–585.
116. Davidson-Methot, David G., "Calibrating the Compass: Using Quality Improvement Data for Outcome Evaluation, Cost Control, and Creating Quality Organizational Cultures," *Residential Treatment for Children & Youth*, Vol. 21, No. 3, 2004, pp. 45–68.
117. Day, George S., "Aligning the Organization with the Market," *MIT Sloan Management Review*, Vol. 48, No. 1, Fall 2006, pp. 41–49.
118. de Vries, Manfred Kets, and Katharina Balazs, "Organizations as Optical Illusions: A Clinical Perspective on Organizational Consultation," *Organizational Dynamics*, Vol. 34, No. 1, 2005, pp. 1–17.
119. DeBode, Jason D., Achilles A. Armenakis, Hubert S. Feild, and Alan G. Walker, "Assessing Ethical Organizational Culture: Refinement of a Scale," *Journal of Applied Behavioral Science*, Vol. 49, No. 4, December 2013, pp. 460–484.
120. DeCelles, Katherine A., Paul E. Tesluk, and Faye S. Taxman, "A Field Investigation of Multilevel Cynicism Toward Change," *Organization Science*, Vol. 24, No. 1, January–February 2013, pp. 154–171.
121. Defense Business Board, "Report to the Secretary of Defense: Innovation and Cultural Change Task Group Report," *Defense Business Board*, May 2006.
122. DeJoy, David M., Lindsay J. Della, Robert J. Vandenberg, and Mark G. Wilson, "Making Work Safer: Testing a Model of Social Exchange and Safety Management," *Journal of Safety Research*, Vol. 41, No. 2, April 2010, pp. 163–171.

123. DeJoy, David M., Mark G. Wilson, Robert J. Vandenberg, Allison L. McGrath-Higgins, and C. Shannon Griffin-Blake, "Assessing the Impact of Healthy Work Organization Intervention," *Journal of Occupational and Organizational Psychology*, Vol. 83,No. 1, March 2010, pp. 139–165.
124. Dellinger, Kirsten, and Christine L. Williams, "The Locker Room and the Dorm Room: Workplace Norms and the Boundaries of Sexual Harassment in Magazine Editing," *Social Problems*, Vol. 49, No. 2, May 2002, pp. 242–257.
125. Deng, Pi-Sheng, "Applying a Market-Based Approach to the Development of a Sharing-Enabled KM Model for Knowledge-Intensive Small Firms," *Information Systems Management*, Vol. 25, No. 2, Spring 2008, pp. 174–187.
126. Denison, Daniel R., "What Is the Difference Between Organizational Culture and Organizational Climate? A Native's Point of View on a Decade of Paradigm Wars," *The Academy of Management Review*, Vol. 21, No. 3, 1996, pp. 619–654.
127. Dennis, Sarah E., and Erin O'Connor, "Reexamining Quality in Early Childhood Education: Exploring the Relationship Between the Organizational Climate and the Classroom," *Journal of Research in Childhood Education*, Vol. 27, No. 1, 2013, pp. 74–92.
128. Devine, Carol M., Janet A. Nelson, Nancy Chin, Ann Dozier, and Isabel Diana Fernandez, "'Pizza Is Cheaper than Salad': Assessing Workers' Views for an Environmental Food Intervention," *Obesity*, Vol. 15, November 2007, pp. 57s–68s.
129. Dextras-Gauthier, Julie, Alain Marchand, and Victor Haines III, "Organizational Culture, Work Organization Conditions, and Mental Health: A Proposed Integration," *International Journal of Stress Management*, Vol. 19, No. 2, May 2012, pp. 81–104.
130. Dickson, Marcus W., D. Brent Smith, Michael W. Grojean, and Mark Ehrhart, "An Organizational Climate Regarding Ethics: The Outcome of Leader Values and the Practices That Reflect Them," *Leadership Quarterly*, Vol. 12, No. 2, Summer 2001, pp. 197–217.
131. Dillon, Bobbie L., "Workplace Violence: Impact, Causes, and Prevention," *Work*, Vol. 42, No. 1, 2012, pp. 15–20.
132. Doherty, Alison, Janet Fink, Sue Inglis, and Donna Pastore, "Understanding a Culture of Diversity Through Frameworks of Power and Change," *Sport Management Review*, Vol. 13, No. 4, November 2010, pp. 368–381.
133. Dombrowski, Caroline, Jeffrey Y. Kim, Kevin C. Desouza, Ashley Braganza, Sridhar Papagari, Peter Baloh, and Sanjeev Jha, "Elements of Innovative Cultures," *Knowledge and Process Management*, Vol. 14, No. 3, July–September 2007, pp. 190–202.
134. Dosoglu-Guner, Berrin, "Can Organizational Behavior Explain the Export Intention of Firms? The Effects of Organizational Culture and Ownership Type," *International Business Review*, Vol. 10, No. 1, 2001, pp. 71–89.
135. Douglass, Anne, and Lorraine Klerman, "The Strengthening Families Initiative and Child Care Quality Improvement: How Strengthening Families Influenced

Change in Child Care Programs in One State," *Early Education and Development*, Vol. 23, No. 3, 2012, pp. 373–392.
136. Duden, Antje, "Trust and Leadership—Learning Culture in Organizations," *International Journal of Management Cases*, January 2011, pp. 218–223.
137. Dufresne, Ronald L., "An Action Learning Perspective on Effective Implementation of Academic Honor Codes," *Group & Organization Management*, Vol. 29, No. 2, April 2004, pp. 201–218.
138. Dull, Matthew, "Leadership and Organizational Culture: Sustaining Dialogue Between Practitioners and Scholars," *Public Administration Review*, Vol. 70, No. 6, November–December 2010, pp. 857–866.
139. Durisin, Boris, and Gergana Todorova, "A Study of the Performativity of the 'Ambidextrous Organizations' Theory: Neither Lost in nor Lost Before Translation," *Journal of Product Innovation Management*, Vol. 29, December 2012, pp. 53–75.
140. Egan, Toby Marshall, Baiyin Yang, and Kenneth R. Bartlett, "The Effects of Organizational Learning Culture and Job Satisfaction on Motivation to Transfer Learning and Turnover Intention," *Human Resource Development Quarterly*, Vol. 15, No. 3., Autumn 2004, pp. 279–301.
141. Ellinger, Alexander E., Carolyn (Casey) Musgrove, Andrea D. Ellinger, Daniel G. Bachrach, Ayşe Banu Elmadağ Baş, and Yu-Lin Wang, "Influences of Organizational Investments in Social Capital on Service Employee Commitment and Performance," *Journal of Business Research*, Vol. 66, No. 8, August 2013, pp. 1124–1133.
142. Ellis, Richard T., *A Method to Determine an Organization's Compatibility with Hybrid Workspaces*, Wright-Patterson Air Force Base, Ohio: Air Force Institute of Technology, 2014.
143. Elmore, Tracey Pemberton, "The Role of Internal Auditors in Creating an Ethical Culture," *Journal of Government Financial Management*, Vol. 62, No. 2, Summer 2013, pp. 48–53.
144. Esaki, Nina, Joseph Benamati, Sarah Yanosy, Jennifer S. Middleton, Laura M. Hopson, Victoria L. Hummer, and Sandra L. Bloom, "The Sanctuary Model: Theoretical Framework," *Families in Society: The Journal of Contemporary Social Services*, Vol. 94, No. 2, April–June 2013, pp. 87–95.
145. Eshbach, Eric C., and James E. Henderson, "The Symbiotic Relationship Between New Principals and the Climate of the Schools in Which They Lead," *e-Journal of Organizational Learning & Leadership*, Vol. 8, No. 1, Spring 2010, pp. 16–48.
146. Eudes, J., "Close the Gap," *Marketing Health Services*, Vol. 26, No. 3, 2006, pp. 32–33.

147. Everly, George S., Jr., Kenneth J. Smith, and Rachel Lobo, "Resilient Leadership and the Organizational Culture of Resilience: Construct Validation," *International Journal of Emergency Mental Health*, Vol. 15, No. 2, 2013, pp. 123–128.
148. Eversole, Barbara A. W., Donald L. Venneberg, and Cindy L. Crowder, "Creating a Flexible Organizational Culture to Attract and Retain Talented Workers Across Generations," *Advances in Developing Human Resources*, Vol. 14, No. 4, November 2012, pp. 607–625.
149. Fauth, James, Sarah Gates, Maria Ann Vinca, Shawna Boles, and Jeffrey A. Hayes, "Big Ideas for Psychotherapy Training," *Psychotherapy: Theory, Research, Practice, Training*, Vol. 44, No. 4, December 2007, pp. 384–391.
150. Fawcett, Stanley E., James C. Brau, Gary K. Rhoads, David Whitlark, and Amydee M. Fawcett, "Spirituality and Organizational Culture: Cultivating the ABCs of an Inspiring Workplace," *International Journal of Public Administration*, Vol. 31, 2008, pp. 420–438.
151. Felblinger, Dianne M., "Incivility and Bullying in the Workplace and Nurses' Shame Responses," *Journal of Obstetric, Gynecologic & Neonatal Nursing*, Vol. 37, No. 2, March–April 2008, pp. 234–242.
152. Feldman, Steven P., "Moral Memory: Why and How Moral Companies Manage Tradition," *Journal of Business Ethics*, Vol. 72, No. 4, June 2007, pp. 395–409.
153. Ferro, Sari, "Creating a Culture of Professional Engagement," *Journal of Jewish Communal Service*, Vol. 85, No. 1, Winter 2010, pp. 195–199.
154. Fink, Regina, Cathy J. Thompson, and Deborah Bonnes, "Overcoming Barriers and Promoting the Use of Research in Practice," *Journal of Nursing Administration*, Vol. 35, No. 3, March 2005, pp. 121–129.
155. Fiume, Orest J., "LEAN at Wiremold: Beyond Manufacturing, Putting People Front and Center," *Journal of Organizational Excellence*, Vol. 23, No. 3, Summer 2004, pp. 23–32.
156. Flores, Luis G., Wei Zheng, Devaki Rau, and Christopher H. Thomas, "Organizational Learning: Subprocess Identification, Construct Validation, and an Empirical Test of Cultural Antecedents," *Journal of Management*, Vol. 38, No. 2, March 2012, pp. 640–667.
157. Foglia, Mary Beth, Jennifer H. Cohen, Robert A. Pearlman, Melissa M. Bottrell, and Ellen Fox, "Perceptions of Ethical Leadership and the Ethical Environment and Culture: IntegratedEthics Staff Survey Data from the VA Health Care System," *The American Journal of Bioethics*, Vol. 4, No. 1, January, 2013, pp. 44–58.
158. Foote, Marianne F., and Wendy E. A. Ruona, "Institutionalizing Ethics: A Synthesis of Frameworks and the Implications for HRD," *Human Resource Development Review*, Vol. 7, No. 3, September 2008, pp. 292–308.

159. Forsythe, Lydia L., "Using an Organizational Culture Analysis to Design Interventions for Change," *AORN Journal*, Vol. 81, No. 6, 2005, pp. 1288, 1290, 1293–1296, 1298, 1301–1302.
160. Fortado, Bruce, and Paul Fadil, "The Four Faces of Organizational Culture," *Competitiveness Review*, Vol. 22, No. 4, 2012, pp. 283–298.
161. Forte, Almerinda, "Business Ethics: A Study of the Moral Reasoning of Selected Business Managers and the Influence of Organizational Ethical Climate," *Journal of Business Ethics*, Vol. 51, No. 2, May 2004, pp. 167–173.
162. France, Daniel J., Robert A. Greevy, Jr., Xulei Liu, Haley Burgess, Robert S. Dittus, Matthew B. Weinger, and Theodore Speroff, "Measuring and Comparing Safety Climate in Intensive Care Units," *Medical Care*, Vol. 48, No. 3, March 2010, pp. 279–284.
163. Frazier, M. Lance, and Stav Fainshmidt, "Voice Climate, Work Outcomes, and the Mediating Role of Psychological Empowerment: A Multilevel Examination," *Group & Organization Management*, Vol. 37, No. 6, December 2012, pp. 691–715.
164. French, Sandra L., and Tracey Quigley Holden, "Positive Organizational Behavior: A Buffer for Bad News," *Business and Professional Communication Quarterly*, Vol. 75, No. 2, June 2012, pp. 208–220.
165. Friday, Earnest, and Shawnta S. Friday, "Managing Diversity Using a Strategic Planned Change Approach," *Journal of Management Development*, Vol. 22, No. 10, 2003, pp. 863–880.
166. Friedberg, Mark William, Dana G. Safran, Kathryn L. Coltin, Marguerite Dresser, and Eric C. Schneider, "Readiness for the Patient-Centered Medical Home: Structural Capabilities of Massachusetts Primary Care Practices," *Journal of General Internal Medicine*, Vol. 24, No. 2, February 2009, pp. 162–169.
167. Froman, Larry, "Positive Psychology in the Workplace," *Journal of Adult Development*, Vol. 17, No. 2, June 2010, pp. 59–69.
168. Frontiera, Joe, "Leadership and Organizational Culture Transformation in Professional Sport," *Journal of Leadership & Organizational Studies*, Vol. 17, No. 1, February 2010, pp. 71–86.
169. Fryer-Edwards, Kelly, Erik Van Eaton, Erika A. Goldstein, Harry R. Kimball, Richard C. Veith, Carlos A. Pellegrini, and Paul G. Ramsey, "Overcoming Institutional Challenges Through Continuous Professionalism Improvement: The University of Washington Experience," *Academic Medicine*, Vol. 82, No. 11, November 2007, pp. 1073–1078.
170. Fuqua, Dale R., and Judy L. Newman, "Creating Caring Organizations," *Consulting Psychology Journal: Practice and Research*, Vol. 54, No. 2, 2002, pp. 131–140.
171. Gadeken, Owen, "The Courage to Raise Your Hand," *Defense AT&L Magazine*, Vol. 39, September–October 2010, pp. 52–54.

172. Gallant, Tricia Bertram, "The Complexity of Integrity Culture Change: A Case Study of a Liberal Arts College," *Review of Higher Education*, Vol. 30, No. 4, Summer 2007, pp. 391–411.
173. Gallus, Jessica A., Jennifer A. Bunk, Russell A. Matthews, Janet L. Barnes-Farrell, and Vicki J. Magley, "An Eye for an Eye? Exploring the Relationship Between Workplace Incivility Experiences and Perpetration," *Journal of Occupational Health Psychology*,Vol. 19, No. 2, April 2014, pp. 143–154.
174. Gandossy, Robert, Rajeev Peshawaria, Leslie Perlow, Fons Trompenaars, and Daisy Wademan Dowling, "Driving Performance Through Corporate Culture: Interviews with Four Experts," *Journal of Applied Corporate Finance*, Vol. 21, No. 2, Spring 2009, pp. 67–73.
175. Garnett, James L., Justin Marlowe, and Sanjay K. Pandey, "Penetrating the Performance Predicament: Communication as a Mediator or Moderator of Organizational Culture's Impact on Public Organizational Performance," *Public Administration Review*, Vol. 68, No. 2, March–April 2008, pp. 266–281.
176. Gebhardt, Gary F., Gregory S. Carpenter, and John F. Sherry, "Creating a Market Orientation: A Longitudinal, Multifirm, Grounded Analysis of Cultural Transformation," *Journal of Marketing*, Vol. 70, No. 4, October, 2006, pp. 37–55.
177. Gebler, David, "Is Your Culture a Risk Factor?" *Business and Society Review*, Vol. 111, No. 3, September 2006, pp. 337–362.
178. Genn, J. M., "AMEE Medical Education Guide No. 23 (Part 2): Curriculum, Environment, Climate, Quality and Change in Medical Education—A Unifying Perspective," *Medical Teacher*, Vol. 23, No. 5, September 2001, pp. 445–454.
179. Giberson, Tomas R., Christian J. Resick, Marcus W. Dickson, Jacqueline K. Mitchelson, Kenneth R. Randall, and Malissa A. Clark, "Leadership and Organizational Culture: Linking CEO Characteristics to Cultural Values," *Journal of Business and Psychology*, Vol. 24, No. 2, June 2009, pp. 123–137.
180. Gibson, Sharon K., "Mentoring of Women Faculty: The Role of Organizational Politics and Culture," *Innovative Higher Education*, Vol. 31, No. 1, June 2006, pp. 63–79.
181. Giffords, Elissa D., and Richard P. Dina, "Changing Organizational Cultures: The Challenge in Forging Successful Mergers," *Administration in Social Work*, Vol. 27, No. 1, 2003, pp. 69–81.
182. Gilmore, Sarah, and Samantha Warren, "Unleashing the Power of the Creative Unconscious Within Organizations: A Case of Craft, Graft and Disputed Premises," *TAMARA: Journal of Critical Postmodern Organization Science*, Vol. 6, No. 1, 2007, pp. 106–122.
183. Givan, Rebecca, "The Maimonides Medical Center Model: Conflict Reduction Through Mutual Respect and Conflict Resolution Through Mediation," *Dispute Resolution Journal*, Vol. 65, No. 4, November–January 2010, p. 11.

184. Glisson, Charles, "The Organizational Context of Children's Mental Health Services," *Clinical Child and Family Psychology Review*, Vol. 5, No. 4, December 2002, pp. 233–253.
185. Glisson, Charles, Denzel Dukes, and Philip Green, "The Effects of the ARC Organizational Intervention on Caseworker Turnover, Climate, and Culture in Children's Service Systems," *Child Abuse & Neglect*, Vol. 30, No. 8, August 2006, pp. 855–880.
186. Glisson, Charles, Anthony Hemmelgarn, Philip Green, Denzel Dukes, Shannon Atkinson, and Nathaniel J. Williams, "Randomized Trial of the Availability, Responsiveness, and Continuity (ARC) Organizational Intervention with Community-Based Mental Health Programs and Clinicians Serving Youth," *Journal of the American Academy of Child & Adolescent Psychiatry*, Vol. 51, No. 8, August 2012, pp. 780–787.
187. Goldman, Ellen F., and Andrea Casey, "Building a Culture that Encourages Strategic Thinking," *Journal of Leadership & Organizational Studies*, Vol. 17, No. 2, 2010, pp. 119–128.
188. Graham, Carrol M., and Fredrick Muyia Nafukho, "Culture, Organizational Learning and Selected Employee Background Variables in Small-Size Business Enterprises," *Journal of European Industrial Training*, Vol. 31, No. 2, 2007, pp. 127–144.
189. Green, Amy E., Brian J. Albanese, Guy Cafri, and Gregory A. Aarons, "Leadership, Organizational Climate, and Working Alliance in a Children's Mental Health Service System," *Community Mental Health Journal*, Vol. 50, No. 7, October 2014, pp. 771–777.
190. Greenberg, Michael D., *Perspectives of Chief Ethics and Compliance Officers on the Detection and Prevention of Corporate Misdeeds: What the Policy Community Should Know*, Santa Monica, Calif.: RAND Corporation, CF-258-RC, 2009.
191. ———, *Corporate Culture and Ethical Leadership Under the Federal Sentencing Guidelines: What Should Boards, Management and Policymakers Do Now?* Santa Monica, Calif.: RAND Corporation, CF-305-CCEG, 2012.
192. ———, *Culture, Compliance, and the C-suite: How Executives, Boards, and Policymakers Can Better Safeguard Against Misconduct at the Top*, Santa Monica, Calif.: RAND Corporation, CF-316-CCEG, 2013.
193. Gregory, Henry Jr., Onna Van Orden, Lisa Jordan, Galina A. Portnoy, Elena Welsh, Jennifer Betkowski, Jade Wolfman Charles, and Carlo C. DiClemente, "New Directions in Capacity Building: Incorporating Cultural Competence into the Interactive Systems Framework," *American Journal of Community Psychology*, Vol. 50, No. 3-4, December 2012, pp. 321–333.
194. Griffin, Marie L., "Job Satisfaction Among Detention Officers—Assessing the Relative Contribution of Organizational Climate Variables," *Journal of Criminal Justice*, Vol. 29, No. 3, May–June 2001, pp. 219–232.

195. Groggins, Ashley, and Ann Marie Ryan, "Embracing Uniqueness: The Underpinnings of a Positive Climate for Diversity," *Journal of Occupational and Organizational Psychology*, Vol. 86, No. 2, June 2014, pp. 264–282.
196. Guldenmund, Frank W., "(Mis)understanding Safety Culture and Its Relationship to Safety Management," *Risk Analysis*, Vol. 30, No. 10, October 2010, pp. 1466–1480.
197. Gunn, Robert A., and Betsy Raskin Gullickson, "Mind-set," *Strategic Finance*, September 1, 2005.
198. Gunn, Vicky, "Mimetic Desire and Intersubjectivity in Disciplinary Cultures: Constraints or Enablers to Learning in Higher Education?" *Studies in Continuing Education*, Vol. 36, No. 1, January 2, 2014, pp. 67–82.
199. Gupta, Vipin, "A Multi-Level Model of Workplace Gender Experience," *Vikalpa: The Journal for Decision Makers*, Vol. 34, No. 4, October 2009, pp. 87–90.
200. Hall, M. Elizabeth Lewis, Brad Christerson, and Shelly Cunningham, "Sanctified Sexism: Religious Beliefs and the Gender Harassment of Academic Women," *Psychology of Women Quarterly*, Vol. 34, No. 2, 2010, pp. 181–185.
201. Hallett, Tim, "Symbolic Power and Organizational Culture," *Sociological Theory*, Vol. 21, No. 2, June 2003, pp. 128–149.
202. Halpern, Janice, Maria Gurevich, Brian Schwartz, and Paulette Brazeau, "Interventions for Critical Incident Stress in Emergency Medical Services: a Qualitative Study," *Stress and Health*, Vol. 25, No. 2, April 2009, pp. 139–149.
203. Hamilton, D. Kirk, Robin Diane Orr, and W. Ellen Raboin, "Organizational Transformation: A Model for Joint Optimization of Culture Change and Evidence-Based Design," *Health Environments Research & Design Journal*, Vol. 1, No. 3, Spring 2008, pp. 40–60.
204. Harrington, Anna, "Affecting the Environment," *Occupational Health*, Vol. 63, No. 2, February 2011, pp. 20–21.
205. Harris, Lloyd C., and Andrew Crane, "The Greening of Organizational Culture—Management Views on the Depth, Degree and Diffusion of Change," *Journal of Organizational Change Management*, Vol. 15, No. 3, 2002, pp. 214–234.
206. Hartmann, Christine W., Mark Meterko, Amy K. Rosen, Zhao Shibei, Priti Shokeen, Sara Singer, and David M. Gaba, "Relationship of Hospital Organizational Culture to Patient Safety Climate in the Veterans Health Administration," *Medical Care Research and Review*, Vol. 66, No. 3, June 2009, pp. 320–338.
207. Hartmann, Jim, and Anne M. Khademian, "Culture Change Refined and Revitalized: The Road Show and Guides for Pragmatic Action," *Public Administration Review*, Vol. 70, No. 6, November–December, 2010, pp. 845–856.
208. Hatch, Mary Jo, and Majken Schultz, "The Dynamics of Organizational Identity," *Human Relations*, Vol. 55, No. 8, August 2002, pp. 989–1018.

209. Hauck, Shella, Rebecca P. Winsett, and Judy Kuric, "Leadership Facilitation Strategies to Establish Evidence-Based Practice in an Acute Care Hospital," *Journal of Advanced Nursing*, Vol. 69, No. 3, March 2013, pp. 664–674.
210. Hays, Paul Sitton, "Narrowing the Gap: Three Key Dimensions of Site-Based Leadership in Four Boston Charter Public Schools," *Education and Urban Society*, Vol. 45, No. 1, January 2013, pp. 37–87.
211. Heckelman, Wendy L., Sheryl Unger, and Christina Garofano, "Driving Culture Transformation During Large-Scale Change," *OD Practitioner*, Vol. 45, No. 3, 2013, pp. 25–30.
212. Heese, Michaela, "Got the Results, Now What Do You Do? Safety Culture Transformation from Theory into Practice," *Aviation Psychology and Applied Human Factors*, Vol. 2, No. 1, 2012, pp. 25–33.
213. Heldenbrand, Lois, and Michael S. Simms, "Missing Link: Integrated Individual Leadership Development, Employee Engagement, and Customer Value-Added Improvement," *Performance Improvement*, Vol. 51, No. 2, February 2012, pp. 28–35.
214. Helfrich, Christian D., Bryan J. Weiner, Martha M. McKinney, and Lori Minasian, "Determinants of Implementation Effectiveness: Adapting a Framework for Complex Innovations," *Medical Care Research and Review*, Vol. 64, No. 3, June 2007, pp. 279–303.
215. Hemmelgarn, Anthony L., Charles Glisson, and Lawrence R. James, "Organizational Culture and Climate: Implications for Services and Interventions Research," *Clinical Psychology-Science and Practice*, Vol. 13, No. 1, Spring 2006, pp. 73–89.
216. Henck, Anita Fitzgerald, "Walking the Tightrope: Christian Colleges and Universities in a Time of Change," *Christian Higher Education*, Vol. 10, No. 3–4, 2011, pp. 196–214.
217. "Henrico County Makes Learning Key to Succession Planning," *Human Resources Department Management Report*, 2008, pp. 1–2.
218. Henry, Linda L., "Disclosure of Medical Errors: Ethical Considerations for the Development of a Facility Policy and Organizational Culture Change," *Policy, Politics, and Nursing Practice*, Vol. 6, No. 2, May 2005, pp. 127–134.
219. Herkenhoff, Linda, "Culturally Tuned Emotional Intelligence: An Effective Change Management Tool?" *Strategic Change*, Vol. 13, No. 2, April 2004, pp. 73–81.
220. Herrera, Richard, Phyllis A. Duncan, Mark Green, Malcom Ree, and Sheryl L. Skaggs, "The Relationship Between Attitudes Toward Diversity Management in the Southwest USA and the GLOBE Study Cultural Preferences," *International Journal of Human Resource Management*, Vol. 22, No. 12, 2011, pp. 2629–2646.

221. Herrera, Richard, Phyllis A. Duncan, Mark T. Green, and Sheryl L. Skaggs, "The Effect of Gender on Leadership and Culture," *Global Business and Organizational Excellence*, Vol. 31, No. 2, 2012, pp. 37–48.
222. Hertzog, Jodie L., David Wright, and Debra Beat, "There's a Policy for That: A Comparison of the Organizational Culture of Workplaces Reporting Incidents of Sexual Harassment," *Behavior and Social Issues*, Vol. 17, No. 2, Fall/Winter 2008, pp. 169–181.
223. Higgins, James M., and Craig Mcallaster, "If You Want Strategic Change, Don't Forget to Change Your Cultural Artifacts," *Journal of Change Management*, Vol. 4, No. 1, 2004, pp. 63–73.
224. Hofmann, David A., and Dov Zohar, "Organizational Culture and Climate," in Steve W. J. Kozlowski, ed., *The Oxford Handbook of Organizational Psychology*, New York: Oxford University Press, 2012.
225. Hogan, Kathleen, "A Sociocultural Analysis of School and Community Settings as Sites for Developing Environmental Practitioners," *Environmental Education Research*, Vol. 8, No. 4, 2002, pp. 413–437.
226. Hogan, Suellen J., and Leonard V. Coote, "Organizational Culture, Innovation, and Performance: A Test of Schein's Model," *Journal of Business Research*, Vol. 67, No. 8, August 2014, pp. 1609–1621.
227. Hopkins, Andrew, "Studying Organisational Cultures and Their Effect on Safety," *Safety Science*, Vol. 44, No. 10, December 2006, pp. 875–889.
228. Hormann, Shana, and Pat Vivian, "Toward an Understanding of Traumatized Organizations and How to Intervene in Them," *Traumatology*, Vol. 11, No. 3, September 2005, pp. 159–169.
229. Horney, Nick, Bill Pasmore, and Tom O'Shea, "Leadership Agility: A Business Imperative for a VUCA World," *People & Strategy*, Vol. 33, No. 4, 2010, pp. 32–38.
230. Houchin, Susan, and Heather Johnston Nicholson, "Holding Ourselves Accountable: Managing by Outcomes in Girls Incorporated," *Nonprofit and Voluntary Sector Quarterly*, Vol. 31, No. 2, June 2002, pp. 271–277.
231. Howard, Carol, Karl Logue, Michelann Quimby, and Jeff Schoeneberg, "Framing Change," *OD Practitioner*, Vol. 41, No. 1, 2009, pp. 25–31.
232. Hoy, Wayne K., Page A. Smith, and Scott R. Sweetland, "The Development of the Organizational Climate Index for High Schools: Its Measure and Relationship to Faculty Trust," *The High School Journal*, Vol. 86, No. 2, December 2002–January 2003, pp. 38–49.
233. Huq, Ziaul, Faizul Huq, and Ken Cutright, "BPR Through ERP: Avoiding Change Management Pitfalls," *Journal of Change Management*, Vol. 6, No. 1, 2006, pp. 67–85.

234. Hyde, Cheryl A., and Aren Hopkins, "Diversity Climates in Human Service Agencies: An Exploratory Assessment," *Journal of Ethnic and Cultural Diversity in Social Work*, Vol. 13, No. 2, 2004, pp. 25–43.
235. Ingram, Thomas N., Raymond W. LaForge, and Charles H. Schwepker, Jr., "Salesperson Ethical Decision Making: The Impact of Sales Leadership and Sales Management Control Strategy," *Journal of Personal Selling & Sales Management*, Vol. 27, No. 4, 2007, pp. 301–315.
236. Interligi, Lisa, "Compliance Culture: A Conceptual Framework," *Journal of Management & Organization*, Vol. 16, No. 2, May 2010, pp. 235–249.
237. Jaffe, Rory S., "The Physician Compensation Plan Affects Organizational Culture," *Journal of Health Care Compliance*, 2002.
238. Jandeska, Kathryn E., and Maria L. Kraimer, "Women's Perceptions of Organizational Culture, Work Attitudes, and Role-Modeling Behaviors," *Journal of Managerial Issues*, Vol. 17, No. 4, Winter 2005, pp. 461–478.
239. Jaskyte, Kristina, "An Exploratory Examination of Correlates of Organizational Culture," *Administration in Social Work*, Vol. 34, No. 5, 2010, pp. 423–441.
240. Jaskyte, Kristina, Christina Byerly, Amanda Bryant, and Julianna Koksarova, "Transforming a Nonprofit Work Environment for Creativity: An Application of Concept Mapping," *Nonprofit Management & Leadership*, Vol. 21, No. 1, Fall 2010, pp. 77–92.
241. Jassawalla, Avan R., and Hemant C. Sashittal, "Cultures That Support Product-Innovation Processes," *Academy of Management Executive*, Vol. 16, No. 3, August 2002, pp. 42–54.
242. Joe, George W., Kirk M. Broome, D. Dwayne Simpson, and Grace A. Rowan-Szal, "Counselor Perceptions of Organizational Factors and Innovations Training Experiences," *Journal of Substance Abuse Treatment*, Vol. 33, No. 2, September 2007, pp. 171–182.
243. Johnson, Barbara H., "EMPOWERMENT of Nurse Educators Through Organizational Culture," *Nursing Education Perspectives*, Vol. 30, No. 1, January–February 2009, pp. 8–13.
244. Johnson, Robin S., "Toward Greater Production Diversity: Examining Social Boundaries at a Video Game Studio," *Games and Culture*, Vol. 8, No. 3, May 2013, pp. 136–160.
245. Johnson, Terrance A., and Raymond W. Cox III, "Police Ethics: Organizational Implications," *Public Integrity*, Vol. 7, No. 1, 2004, pp. 67–79.
246. Johnson-Cramer, Michael E., Salvatore Parise, and Robert L. Cross, "Managing Change Through Networks and Values," *California Management Review*, Vol. 49, No. 3, Spring 2007, pp. 85–109.
247. Jolink, Mark, and Ben Dankbaar, "Creating a Climate for Inter-Organizational Networking Through People Management," *International Journal of Human Resource Management*, Vol. 21, No. 9, 2010, pp. 1436–1453.

248. Jonas, Wayne, Patricia Deuster, Francis O'Connor, and Christina Macedonia, "Total Force Fitness for the 21st Century: A New Paradigm," *Samueli Institute*, Vol. 175, Suppl., August 2010.
249. Jones, Janice M., "Dual or Dueling Culture and Commitment: The Impact of a Tri-Hospital Merger," *Journal of Nursing Administration*, Vol. 33, No. 4, April 2003, pp. 235–242.
250. Jones, Mark Peter, "Networked Success and Failure at Hybritech," *Bulletin of Science, Technology & Society*, Vol. 31, No. 6, December 2011, pp. 448–459.
251. Jordan, Neil, Scott C. Leon, Richard A. Epstein, Elizabeth Durkin, Jena Helgerson, and Brittany L. Lakin, "Effect of Organizational Climate on Youth Outcomes in Residential Treatment," *Residential Treatment for Children & Youth*, Vol. 26, No. 3, 2009, pp. 194–208.
252. Kaarst-Brown, Michelle L., Scott Nicholson, Gisela M. von Dran, and Jeffrey M. Stanton, "Organizational Cultures of Libraries as a Strategic Resource," *Library Trends*, Vol. 53, No. 1, Summer 2004, pp. 33–53.
253. Kaliprasad, Minnesh, "The Human Factor II: Creating a High Performance Culture in an Organization," *Cost Engineering*, Vol. 48, No. 6, 2006, pp. 27–34.
254. Kampas, P. J., "Shifting Cultural Gears in Technology-Driven Industries," *MIT Sloan Management Review*, Vol. 44, No. 2, Winter 2003, pp. 41–48.
255. Kaptein, Muel, "The Ethics of Organizations: A Longitudinal Study of the U.S. Working Population," *Journal of Business Ethics*, Vol. 92, No. 4, April 2010, pp. 601–618.
256. Kash, Bita Arbab, Aaron Spaulding, Christopher E. Johnson, and Larry Gamm, "Success Factors for Strategic Change Initiatives: A Qualitative Study of Healthcare Administrators' Perspectives," *Journal of Healthcare Management*, Vol. 59, No. 1, January–February 2013, pp. 65–81.
257. Kayes, D. Christopher, David Stirling, and Tjai M. Nielsen, "Building Organizational Integrity," *Business Horizons*, Vol. 50, 2007, pp. 61–70.
258. Keenan, John P., "Whistleblowing: A Study of Managerial Differences," *Employee Responsibilities and Rights Journal*, Vol. 14, No. 1, March 2002, pp. 17–32.
259. Kellogg, Katherine C., "Hot Lights and Cold Steel: Cultural and Political Toolkits for Practice Change in Surgery," *Organization Science*, Vol. 22, No. 2, March–April 2011, pp. 482–502.
260. Kelly, Erin L., Samantha K. Ammons, Kelly Chermack, and Phyllis Moen, "Gendered Challenge, Gendered Response: Confronting the Ideal Worker Norm in a White-Collar Organization," *Gender & Society*, Vol. 24, No. 3, May 1, 2010, pp. 281–303.
261. Kelly, Patrick T., and Christine E. Earley, "Leadership and Organizational Culture: Lessons Learned from Arthur Andersen," *Accounting and the Public Interest*, Vol. 9, No. 1, December 2009, pp. 129–147.

262. Kenny, Deborah J., Maggie L. Richard, Xochitl Ceniceros, and Kelli Blaize, "Collaborating Across Services to Advance Evidence-Based Nursing Practice," *Nursing Research*, Vol. 59, No. 1, Supp., January–February 2010, pp. S11–S21.
263. Kezar, Adrianna, "Institutionalizing Student Outcomes Assessment: The Need for Better Research to Inform Practice," *Innovative Higher Education*, Vol. 38, No. 3, June 2013, pp. 189–206.
264. Kezar, Adrianna J., *Understanding and Facilitating Organizational Change in the 21st Century: Recent Research and Conceptualizations*, San Francisco: Jossey-Bass, 2001.
265. Khatri, Naresh, Gordon D. Brown, and Lanis L. Hicks, "From a Blame Culture to a Just Culture in Health Care," *Health Care Management Review*, Vol. 34, No. 4, October–December 2009, pp. 312–322.
266. Khazanchi, Shalini, Marianne W. Lewis, and Kenneth K. Boyer, "Innovation-Supportive Culture: The Impact of Organizational Values on Process Innovation," *Journal of Operations Management*, Vol. 25, No. 4, June 2007, pp. 871–884.
267. Khoja, Faiza, "The Triad: Organizational Cultural Values, Practices and Strong Social Intra-Firm Networks," *Journal of Business Strategies*, Vol. 27, No. 2, Fall 2010, pp. 205–228.
268. King, Eden B., Michelle R. Hebl, Jennifer M. George, and Sharon F. Matusik, "Understanding Tokenism: Antecedents and Consequences of a Psychological Climate of Gender Inequity," *Journal of Management*, Vol. 36, No. 2, March 10, 2010, pp. 482–510.
269. Kingshott, Brian, "Women in Policing: Changing the Organizational Culture by Adopting a Feminist Perspective on Leadership," *Criminal Justice Studies: A Critical Journal of Crime, Law & Society*, Vol. 22, No. 1, 2009, pp. 49–72.
270. Kirby, Sheila Nataraj, Julie A. Marsh, Jennifer Sloan McCombs, Harry J. Thie, Nailing Xia, and Jerry M. Sollinger, *Developing Military Health Care Leaders: Insights from the Military, Civilian, and Government Sectors*, Santa Monica, Calif.: RAND Corporation, 2011.
271. Kirby, Sheila Nataraj, Julie A. Marsh, and Harry J. Thie, *Establishing a Research and Evaluation Capability for the Joint Medical Education and Training Campus*, Santa Monica, Calif.: RAND Corporation, 2011.
272. Kirby, Sheila Nataraj, Jennifer Sloan McCombs, Heather Barney, and Scott Naftel, *Reforming Teacher Education: Something Old, Something New*, Santa Monica, Calif.: RAND Corporation, MG-506-EDU, 2006.
273. Kirca, Ahmet H., S. Tarner Cavusgil, and G. Tomas M. Hult, "The Effects of National Culture on Market Orientation: Conceptual Framework and Research Propositions," *International Business Review*, Vol. 18, No. 2, April 2009, pp. 111–118.
274. Kirschbaum, Kristen A., John P. Rask, Matthew Brennan, Sharon Phelan, and Sally A. Fortner, "Improved Climate, Culture, and Communication Through

Multidisciplinary Training and Instruction," *American Journal of Obstetrics and Gynecology*, Vol. 207, No. 3, September 2012, pp. 200.e1–200.e7.

275. Klein, Andrew, "Corporate Culture: Its Value as a Resource for Competitive Advantage," *Journal of Business Strategy*, Vol. 32, No. 2, 2011, pp. 21–28.
276. Klenke, Karin, "Corporate Values as Multi-Level, Multi-Domain Antecedents of Leader Behaviors," *International Journal of Manpower*, Vol. 26, No. 1, 2005, pp. 50–66.
277. Knudsen, Hannah K., Lori J. Ducharme, and Paul M. Roman, "Counselor Emotional Exhaustion and Turnover Intention in Therapeutic Communities," *Journal of Substance Abuse Treatment*, Vol. 31, No. 2, September 2006, pp. 173–180.
278. Koall, Iris, "Managing Complexity: Using Ambivalence and Contingency to Support Diversity in Organizations," *Equality, Diversity & Inclusion*, Vol. 30, No. 7, 2011, pp. 572–588.
279. Koch, Hope, Dorothy E. Leidner, and Ester S. Gonzalez, "Digitally Enabling Social Networks: Resolving IT-Culture Conflict," *Information Systems Journal*, Vol. 23, No. 6, 2013.
280. Kodali, Bhavani S., Dennie Kim, Ronald Bleday, Hugh Flanagan, and Richard D. Urman, "Successful Strategies for the Reduction of Operating Room Turnover Times in a Tertiary Care Academic Medical Center," *Journal of Surgical Research*, Vol. 187, No. 2, April 2014, pp. 403–411.
281. Kondra, Alex Z., and Deborah C. Hurst, "Institutional Processes of Organizational Culture," *Culture and Organization*, Vol. 15, No. 1, 2009, pp. 39–58.
282. Koppes, Laura L., "Facilitating an Organization to Embrace a Work-Life Effectiveness Culture: A Practical Approach," *Psychologist-Manager Journal*, Vol. 11, No. 1, 2008, pp. 163–184.
283. Kossek, Ellen E., Leslie B. Hammer, Erin L. Kelly, and Phyllis Moen, "Designing Work, Family & Health Organizational Change Initiatives," *Organizational Dynamics*, Vol. 43, No. 1, 2014, pp. 53–63.
284. Kotrba, Lindsey M., Michael A. Gillespie, Aaron M. Schmidt, Ryan E. Smerek, Samanth A. Ritchie, and Daniel R. Denison, "Do Consistent Corporate Cultures Have Better Business Performance? Exploring the Interaction Effects," *Human Relations*, Vol. 65, No. 2, 2012, pp. 241–262.
285. Kotzian, Mike, "Leadership and Cultural Change: The Challenge to Acquisition Workforce Retention," *Defense AR Journal*, Vol. 16, No. 1, 2009, pp. 32–52.
286. Koutroumanis, Dean A., and George Alexakis, "Organizational Culture in the Restaurant Industry: Implications for Change," *Journal of Organizational Culture, Communications and Conflict*, Vol. 13, No. 2, July 2009, pp. 45–55.
287. Kralewski, John, Bryan E. Dowd, Amer Kaissi, Ann Curoe, and Todd Rockwood, "Measuring the Culture of Medical Group Practices," *Health Care Manage Review*, Vol. 30, No. 3, July–September 2005, pp. 184–193.

288. Krause, Thomas R., "Influencing the Behavior of Senior Leadership," *Professional Safety*, Vol. 49, No. 6, June 2004, pp. 29–31.
289. Krull, Ivy, Lena Lundgren, and Cielia Beltrame, "Association Between Addiction Treatment Staff Professional and Educational Levels and Perceptions of Organizational Climate and Resources," *Substance Abuse*, Vol. 35, No. 1, January 1, 2014, pp. 3–6.
290. Krupat, Edward, Linda Pololi, Eugene R. Schnell, and David E. Kern, "Changing the Culture of Academic Medicine: The C-Change Learning Action Network and Its Impact at Participating Medical Schools," *Academic Medicine*, Vol. 88, No. 9, September 2013, pp. 1252–1258.
291. Kujala, Jaakko, "Total Quality Management as a Cultural Phenomenon," *Quality Management Journal*, Vol. 11, No. 4, 2004, pp. 43–55.
292. Kulas, John T., Joanne E. McInnerney, Rachel F. DeMuth, and Victoria Jadwinski, "Employee Satisfaction and Theft: Testing Climate Perceptions as a Mediator," *Journal of Psychology*, Vol. 141, No. 4, Jul, 2007, pp. 389–402.
293. Kundu, Kaushik, "Influence of Organizational Culture on the Institution Building Process of an Organization," *CURIE Journal*, Vol. 2, No. 4, January, 2010, pp. 48–57.
294. Kusy, Mitchell, and Elizabeth L. Holloway, "A Field Guide to Real-Time Culture Change: Just Rolling Out a Training Program Won't Cut It," *Journal of Medical Practice Management*, Vol. 29, No. 5, March–April 2014, pp. 294–303.
295. Lampe, Anna Carol, "The Silencing of Voices: The Corporate 'Darkness' Nobody Hears," *Culture and Organization*, Vol. 8, No. 2, 2002, pp. 129–144.
296. Larrison, Christopher R., Susan Schoppelrey, Eric Hadley-Ives, and Barry J. Ackerson, "Organizational Climate and Treatment Outcomes for African American Clients Receiving Services at Community Mental Health Agencies," *Administration in Social Work*, Vol. 32, No. 3, 2008, pp. 111–138.
297. Larson, John, and Brian H. Kleiner, "How to Read Non Verbal Communication in Organisations," *Management Research News*, Vol. 27, No. 4/5, 2004, pp. 17–22.
298. Latham, John, "A Framework for Leading the Transformation to Performance Excellence Part I: CEO Perspectives on Forces, Facilitators, and Strategic Leadership Systems," *Quality Management Journal*, Vol. 20, No. 3, 2013, pp. 19–40.
299. Latta, Gail F., "A Process Model of Organizational Change in Cultural Context (OC3 Model): The Impact of Organizational Culture on Leading Change," *Journal of Leadership & Organizational Studies*, Vol. 16, No. 1, August 2009, pp. 19–37.
300. "Leading People Through Change: How to Manage Your Most Valuable Asset," *Strategic Direction*, Vol. 23, No. 5, 2007, pp. 20–23.
301. Leavy, Brian, "A Leader's Guide to Creating an Innovation Culture," *Strategy & Leadership*, Vol. 33, No. 4, 2005, pp. 38–45.

302. Lee, Ji-Eun, Barbara A. Almanza, SooCheong (Shawn) Jang, Douglas C. Nelson, and Richard F. Ghiselli, "Does Transformational Leadership Style Influence Employees' Attitudes Toward Food Safety Practices?" *International Journal of Hospitality Management*, Vol. 33, June 2013, pp. 282–293.
303. Lee, Jenny J., Leticia Oseguera, Karen A. Kim, Amy Fann, Tracy M. Davis, and Robert A. Rhoads, "Tangles in the Tapestry: Cultural Barriers to Graduate Student Unionization," *Journal of Higher Education*, Vol. 75, No. 3, May–June 2004, pp. 340–361.
304. Lehman, Wayne E., Jack M. Greener, and D. Dwayne Simpson, "Assessing Organizational Readiness for Change," *Journal of Substance Abuse Treatment*, Vol. 22, No. 4, June 2002, pp. 197–209.
305. Lei, David, and Charles R. Greer, "The Empathetic Organization," *Organizational Dynamics*, Vol. 32, No. 2, 2003, pp. 142–164.
306. Lemon, M., and P. S. Sahota, "Organizational Culture as a Knowledge Repository for Increased Innovative Capacity," *Technovation*, Vol. 24, No. 6, June 2004, pp. 483–498.
307. Leonard, Elisabeth, and Betsy Clementson, "Business Librarians and Entrepreneurship: Innovation Trends and Characteristics," *New Review of Information Networking*, Vol. 17, No. 1, 2012, pp. 1–21.
308. Levine, Roger, Darlene Russ-Eft, Andrea Burling, Jennifer Stephens, and Joanna Downey, "Evaluating Health Services Research Capacity Building Programs: Implications for Health Services and Human Resource Development," *Evaluation and Program Planning*, Vol. 37, April 2013, pp. 1–11.
309. Lindberg, Arley, and Larry Meredith, "Building a Culture of Learning Through Organizational Development: The Experiences of the Marin County Health and Human Services Department," *Journal of Evidence-Based Social Work*, Vol. 9, No. 1–2, 2012, pp. 27–42.
310. Linnean, Harold W. III, *Air Force Smart Operations for the Twenty-First Century: Identifying Potential Failure Points in Sustaining Continuous Process Improvement Across the Air Force*, Maxwell Air Force Base, Ala.: Air University, 2007.
311. Linnenluecke, Martina K., and Andrew Griffiths, "Corporate Sustainability and Organizational Culture," *Journal of World Business*, Vol. 45, No. 4, October 2010, pp. 357–366.
312. Listyowardojo, Tita A., Raoul E. Nap, and Addie Johnson, "Variations in Hospital Worker Perceptions of Safety Culture," *International Journal for Quality in Health Care*, Vol. 24, No. 1, February 2012, pp. 9–15.
313. Livingood, William C., Radwan Sabbagh, Steve Spitzfaden, Angela Hicks, Lucy Wells, Suzannah Puigdomenech, Dale F. Kramer, Ryan Butterfield, William Riley, and David L. Wood, "A Quality Improvement Evaluation Case Study: Impact on Public Health Outcomes and Agency Culture," *American Journal of Preventive Medicine*, Vol. 44, No. 5, May 2013, pp. 445–452.

314. Lucas, Henry C., and Jie Mein Goh, "Disruptive Technology: How Kodak Missed the Digital Photography Revolution," *Journal of Strategic Information Systems*, Vol. 18, No. 1, March 2009, pp. 46–55.
315. Lucier, Kathleen H., "A Consultative Training Program: Collateral Effect of a Needs Assessment," Communication Education, Vol. 57, No. 4, October 2008, pp. 482–489.
316. Lurie, Irene, and Norma M. Riccucci, "Changing the 'Culture' of Welfare Offices—From Vision to the Front Lines," *Administration & Society*, Vol. 34, No. 6, January 2003, pp. 653–677.
317. Luxford, Karen, Dana Gelb Safran, and Tom Delbanco, "Promoting Patient-Centered Care: A Qualitative Study of Facilitators and Barriers in Healthcare Organizations with a Reputation for Improving the Patient Experience," *International Journal for Quality in Health Care*, Vol. 23, No. 5, October 2011, pp. 510–515.
318. Lyon, David, "How Can You Help Organizations Change to Meet the Corporate Responsibility Agenda?" *Corporate Social Responsibility and Environmental Management*, Vol. 11, No. 3, 2004, pp. 133–139.
319. Lyons, Stacie Salsbury, "How Do People Make Continence Care Happen? An Analysis of Organizational Culture in Two Nursing Homes," *Gerontologist*, Vol. 50, No. 3,June 2010, pp. 327–339.
320. MacLean, Tammy L., "Framing and Organizational Misconduct: A Symbolic Interactionist Study," *Journal of Business Ethics*, Vol. 78, No. 1–2, March 2008, pp. 3–16.
321. Madsen, Susan, and Charles Vance, "Unlearned Lessons from the Past: An Insider's View of Enron's Downfall," *Corporate Governance: The International Journal of Effective Board Performance*, Vol. 9, No. 2, 2009, pp. 216–227.
322. Mahnken, Thomas G., and James R. Fitzsimonds, "Tread-Heads or Technophiles? Army Officer Attitudes Toward Transformation," *Parameters*, Vol. 34, No. 2, Summer 2004, pp. 57–72.
323. Maignan, Isabelle, Tracy L. Gonzalez-Padron, G. Thomas M. Hult, and O. C. Ferrell, "Stakeholder Orientation: Development and Testing of a Framework for Socially Responsible Marketing," *Journal of Strategic Marketing*, Vol. 19, No. 4, 2011, pp. 313–338.
324. Mallak, Larry, "Understanding and Changing Your Organization's Culture," *Industrial Management*, Vol. 43, No. 2, March/April 2001, pp. 18–24.
325. Mallak, Larry A., and D. M. Lyth, "Using Desired Culture Analysis to Manage Decentralized Operations," *Engineering Management Journal*, Vol. 21, No. 2, June 2009, pp. 27–32.
326. Maloney, Krisellen, Kristin Antelman, Kenning Arlitsch, and John Butler, "Future Leaders' Views on Organizational Culture," *College & Research Libraries*, Vol. 71, No. 4, July 2010, pp. 322–345.

327. Mannan, M. Sam, Ray A. Mentzer, and Jiaqi Zhang, "Framework for Creating a Best-in-Class Safety Culture," *Journal of Loss Prevention in the Process Industries*, Vol. 26, No. 6, November 2013, pp. 1423–1432.
328. Mantel, Jessica, "The Myth of the Independent Physician: Implications for Health Law, Policy, and Ethics," *Case Western Reserve Law Review*, Vol. 64, No. 2, Winter 2013, pp. 455–521.
329. Mărăcine, Mihaela Simona, "Organizational Culture: Basic Element of Organization Performance," *Young Economists Journal/Revista Tinerilor Economisti*, Vol. 9, No. 18, April 2012, pp. 149–156.
330. Markham, Stephen K., and Hyunjung Lee, "Use of an Innovation Board to Integrate the Front End of Innovation with Formal NDP Processes," *Research-Technology Management*, Vol. 56, No. 4, July–August 2013, pp. 37–44.
331. Marquis, Jefferson P., Nelson Lim, Lynn M. Scott, Margaret C. Harrell, and Jennifer Kavanagh, *Managing Diversity in Corporate America: An Exploratory Analysis*, Santa Monica, Calif.: RAND Corporation, P-206-RC, 2008.
332. Martin, Thomas N., and Ziaul Huq, "A Hospital Case Study Supporting Workforce Culture Re-engineering," *Total Quality Management*, Vol. 13, No. 4, July 2002, pp. 523–536.
333. Martins, Luis L., "Organizational Change and Development," in Sheldon Zedeck, ed., *APA Handbook of Industrial and Organizational Psychology*, Washington, D.C.: American Psychological Association, 2011.
334. Mateiu, Sergiu, Vasile Puiu, and George-Constantin Puiu, "A Possible Design Model of the Organizational Culture," *Land Forces Academy Review*, Vol. 18, No. 2, December 2013,pp. 171–175.
335. Mawritz, Mary B., Scott B. Dust, and Christian J. Resick, "Hostile Climate, Abusive Supervision, and Employee Coping: Does Conscientiousness Matter?" *Journal of Applied Psychology*, Vol. 99, No. 4, July 2014, pp. 737–747.
336. Mayer, Celeste M., and Dale Cronin, "Organizational Accountability in a Just Culture," *Urologic Nursing*, Vol. 28, No. 6, January 2009, pp. 427–430.
337. Mazutis, Daina, and Natalie Slawinski, "Leading Organizational Learning Through Authentic Dialogue," *Management Learning*, Vol. 39, No. 4, September 2008, pp. 437–456.
338. McCarthy, Douglas, and David Blumenthal, "Stories from the Sharp End: Case Studies in Safety Improvement," *Milbank Quarterly*, Vol. 84, No. 1, 2006, pp. 165–200.
339. McGuire, John B., Gary Rhodes, and Charles J. Palus, "Inside Out: Transforming Your Leadership Culture," *Leadership in Action*, Vol. 26, No. 7, January/February 2008, pp. 3–7.
340. McKay, Patrick F., Derek R. Avery, and Mark A. Morris, "A Tale of Two Climates: Diversity Climate from Subordinates' and Managers' Perspectives and Their Role

in Store Unit Sales Performance," *Personnel Psychology*, Vol. 62, No. 4, Winter 2009, pp. 767–791.
341. McLean, Laird D., "Organizational Culture's Influence on Creativity and Innovation: A Review of the Literature and Implications for Human Resource Development," *Advances in Developing Human Resources*, Vol. 7, No. 2, May 2005, pp. 226–246.
342. Meancy, Mark E., "Error Reduction, Patient Safety and Institutional Ethics Committees," *Journal of Law, Medicine & Ethics*, Vol. 32, No. 2, Summer 2004, pp. 358–364.
343. Meléndez, Juan, "Distance Education: The Experience of the University of Puerto Rico/Río Piedras Campus," *Higher Education in Europe*, Vol. 26, December 2001, pp. 537–540.
344. Melnick, Gerald, Wendy R. Ulaszek, Hsiu-Ju Lin, and Harry K. Wexler, "When Goals Diverge: Staff Consensus and the Organizational Climate," *Drug and Alcohol Dependence*, Vol. 103, Supplement 1, August 1, 2009, pp. S17–S22.
345. Melton, E. Nicole, and George B. Cunningham, "Who Are the Champions? Using a Multilevel Model to Examine Perceptions of Employee Support for LGBT Inclusion in Sport Organizations," *Journal of Sport Management*, Vol. 28, No. 2, March 2014, pp. 189–206.
346. Merton, Prudence, "A Case Study of Relationships Between Organizational Culture and Curricular Change in Engineering Education," *Innovative Higher Education*, Vol. 34, No. 4, 2009, pp. 219–233.
347. Meyers, Christopher, "Institutional Culture and Individual Behavior: Creating an Ethical Environment," *Science and Engineering Ethics*, Vol. 10, No. 2, April 2004, pp. 269–276.
348. Michalak, Sarah C., "This Changes Everything: Transforming the Academic Library," *Journal of Library Administration*, Vol. 52, No. 5, 2012, pp. 411–423.
349. Michel, John W., Michael J. Kavanagh, and J. Bruce Tracey, "Got Support? The Impact of Supportive Work Practices on the Perceptions, Motivation, and Behavior of Customer-Contact Employees," *Cornell Hospitality Quarterly*, Vol. 54, No. 2, May 2013, pp. 161–173.
350. Mike, Barry, and John W. Slocum, Jr., "Slice of Reality: Changing Culture at Pizza Hut and Yum! Brands, Inc.," *Organizational Dynamics*, Vol. 32, No. 4, 2003, pp. 319–330.
351. Mills, Ann E., Mary V. Rorty, and Patricia H. Werhane, "Complexity and the Role of Ethics in Health Care," *Emergence*, Vol. 5, No. 3, 2003, pp. 6–21.
352. Mills, Peter, Julia Neily, and Ed Dunn, "Teamwork and Communication in Surgical Teams: Implications for Patient Safety," *Journal of the American College of Surgeons*, Vol. 206, No. 1, January 2008, pp. 107–112.

353. Minor, James T., and William G. Tierney, "The Danger of Deference: A Case of Polite Governance," *Teachers College Record*, Vol. 107, No. 1, January 2005, pp. 137–156.
354. Mitchell, Regina L. Garza, "Online Education and Organizational Change," *Community College Review*, Vol. 37, No. 1, July 2009, pp. 81–101.
355. Moon, Henry, Ephrat Livne, and Sophia Marinova, "Understanding the Independent Influence of Duty and Achievement Striving When Predicting the Relationship Between Conscientiousness and Organizational Cultural Profiles and Helping Behaviors," *Journal of Personality Assessment*, Vol. 95, No. 2, March 1, 2013, pp. 225–232.
356. Moore, Jo Ellen, and Lisa A. Burke, "How to Turn Around 'Turnover Culture' in IT," *Communications of the ACM*, Vol. 45, No. 2, February 2002, pp. 73–78.
357. Morris, Anne, and Joan R. Bloom, "Contextual Factors Affecting Job Satisfaction and Organizational Commitment in Community Mental Health Centers Undergoing System Changes in the Financing of Care," *Mental Health Services Research*, Vol. 4,No. 2, June 2002, pp. 71–83.
358. Mouton, Nico, Sine Nørholm Just, and Jonas Gabrielsen, "Creating Organizational Cultures: Re-conceptualizing the Relations Between Rhetorical Strategies and Material Practices," *Journal of Organizational Change Management*, Vol. 25, No. 2, 2012, pp. 315–331.
359. Moynihan, Donald P., and Sanjay K. Pandey, "Testing How Management Matters in an Era of Government by Performance Management," *Journal of Public Administration Research and Theory*, Vol. 15, No. 3, July 2005, pp. 421–439.
360. Moynihan, Donald P., Sanjay K. Pandey, and Bradley E. Wright, "Setting the Table: How Transformational Leadership Fosters Performance Information Use," *Journal of Public Administration Research and Theory*, Vol. 22, No. 1, January 2012, pp. 143–164.
361. Munroe, Donna J., Poonam L. Kaza, and David Howard, "Culture-Change Training: Nursing Facility Staff Perceptions of Culture Change," *Geriatric Nursing*, Vol. 32, No. 6, November–December 2011, pp. 400–407.
362. Murphy, Joseph, Stephen N. Elliott, Ellen Goldring, and Andrew C. Porter, "Leadership for Learning: A Research-Based Model and Taxonomy of Behaviors," *School Leadership & Management*, Vol. 27, No. 2, April 2007, pp. 179–201.
363. Murrow, J., P. Nowak, and W. S. Hurst, "To Protect and Preserve. Can Switching Costs Help the Physician Shortage?" *Marketing Health Services*, Vol. 27, No. 2, Summer 2007, pp. 22–25.
364. Nahm, Abraham Y., Mark A. Vonderembse, and Xenophon A. Koufteros, "The Impact of Organizational Culture on Time-Based Manufacturing and Performance," *Decision Sciences*, Vol. 35, No. 4, Fall 2004, pp. 579–607.

365. Narine, L., and D. D. Persaud, "Gaining and Maintaining Commitment to Large-Scale Change in Healthcare Organizations," *Health Services Management Research*, Vol. 16, No. 3, August 2003, pp. 179–187.
366. National Defense Research Institute, *Sexual Orientation and US Military Personnel Policy: An Update of RAND's 1993 Study*, Santa Monica, Calif.: RAND Corporation, MG-1056-OSD, 2010.
367. Nembhard, Ingrid M., Veronika Northrup, Dale Shaller, and Paul D. Cleary, "Improving Organizational Climate for Quality and Quality of Care: Does Membership in a Collaborative Help?" *Medical Care*, Vol. 50, Supp., November 2012, pp. S74–S82.
368. Nembhard, Ingrid M., Sara J. Singer, Stephen M. Shortell, Diane Rittenhouse, and Lawrence P. Casalino, "The Cultural Complexity of Medical Groups," *Health Care Manage Review*, Vol. 37, No. 3, July–September 2012, pp. 200–213.
369. Nemec, Patricia B., "Developing an Integrated Workforce Development Plan," *Psychiatric Rehabilitation Journal*, Vol. 35, No. 4, Spring 2012, pp. 351–354.
370. Nica, Elvira, "Organizational Culture in the Public Sector," *Economics, Management and Financial Markets*, Vol. 8, No. 2, February 2013, pp. 179–184.
371. Nielsen, Suzanne C., *An Army Transformed: The US Army's Post-Vietnam Recovery and the Dynamics of Change in Military Organizations*, Carlisle, Pa.: U.S. Army War College, 2010.
372. Nieminen, Levi, Benjamin Biermeier-Hanson, and Daniel Denison, "Aligning Leadership and Organizational Culture: The Leader-Culture Fit Framework for Coaching Organizational Leaders," *Consulting Psychology Journal: Practice and Research*, Vol. 65, No. 3, September 2013, pp. 177–198.
373. Nieva, V. F., and J. Sorra, "Safety Culture Assessment: A Tool for Improving Patient Safety in Healthcare Organizations," *Quality & Safety in Health Care*, Vol. 12, Supp. 2, December 2003, pp. ii17–ii23.
374. Nissley, Nick, "Tuning-In to Organizational Song as Aesthetic Discourse," *Culture and Organization*, Vol. 8, No. 1, 2002, pp. 51–68.
375. Nold, Herbert A., III, "Linking Knowledge Processes with Firm Performance: Organizational Culture," *Journal of Intellectual Capital*, Vol. 13, No. 1, 2012, pp. 16–38.
376. Norton, Thomas, Hannes Zacher, and Neal M. Ashkanasy, "On the Importance of Pro-Environmental Organizational Climate for Employee Green Behavior," *Industrial and Organizational Psychology: Perspectives on Science and Practice*, Vol. 5, No. 4, 2012, pp. 497–500.
377. Novicoff, Wendy M., and Scott McMeans, "Prescription for Innovation at Holy Family Memorial: Make Big Progress by Thinking Small," *Global Business and Organizational Excellence*, Vol. 31, No. 3, 2012, pp. 23–31.

378. Nowinski, Cindy J., Susan M. Becker, Katherine S. Reynolds, Jennifer L. Beaumont, Carol Ann Caprini, Elizabeth A. Hahn, Alan Peres, and Benjamin J. Arnold, "The Impact of Converting to an Electronic Health Record on Organizational Culture and Quality Improvement," *International Journal of Medical Informatics*, Vol. 76, Supp. 1, June 2007, pp. S174–S183.
379. Nuckols, Teryl K., Douglas S. Bell, Susan M. Paddock, and Lee H. Hilborne, "Comparing Process- and Outcome-Oriented Approaches to Voluntary Incident Reporting in Two Hospitals," *Joint Commission Journal on Quality and Patient Safety*, Vol. 35, No. 3, March 2009, pp. 139–145.
380. Obenchain, Alice M., William C. Johnson, and Paul A. Dion, "Institutional Types, Organizational Cultures, and Innovation in Christian Colleges and Universities," *Christian Higher Education*, Vol. 3, No. 1, January–March 2004, pp. 15–39.
381. Offstein, Evan H., and Ronald L. Dufresne, "Building Strong Ethics and Promoting Positive Character Development: The Influence of HRM at the United States Military Academy at West Point," *Human Resource Management*, Vol. 46, No. 1, Spring 2007, pp. 95–114.
382. Ogiehor-Enoma, Grace, Leila Taqueban, and Agatha Anosike, "6 Steps for Transforming Organizational EBP Culture," *Nursing Management*, Vol. 41, No. 5, May 2010, pp. 14–17.
383. Ohlinger, Judy, Mark S. Brown, Sue Laudert, Sue Swanson, and Ona Fofah, "Development of Potentially Better Practices for the Neonatal Intensive Care Unit as a Culture of Collaboration: Communication, Accountability, Respect, and Empowerment," *Pediatrics*, Vol. 111, No. 4, April 2003.
384. Olive, Claire, T. Michael O'Connor, and M. Sam Mannan, "Relationship of Safety Culture and Process Safety," *Journal of Hazardous Materials*, Vol. 130, No. 1–2, March 17, 2006, pp. 133–140.
385. Ondeck, Deborah Mariano, "Culture Change: Is It Possible?," *Home Health Care Management & Practice*, Vol. 15, No. 6, October 2003, pp. 525–526.
386. Park, Kyoung-Ok, Bryan S. Schaffer, C. Shannon Griffin-Blake, David M. Dejoy, Mark G. Wilson, and Robert J. Vandenberg, "Effectiveness of a Healthy Work Organization Intervention: Ethic Group Differences," *Journal of Occupational & Environmental Medicine*, Vol. 46, No. 7, 2004, pp. 623–634.
387. Parker, Barbara, and John W. Selsky, "Interface Dynamics in Cause-Based Partnerships: An Exploration of Emergent Culture," *Nonprofit and Voluntary Sector Quarterly*, Vol. 33, No. 3, September 2004, pp. 458–488.
388. Parks, Kizzy M., Stephen B. Knouse, Loring J. Crepeau, and Daniel P. McDonald, "Latina Perceptions of Diversity Climate in the Military," *Business Journal of Hispanic Research*, Vol. 2, 2008, pp. 48–61.
389. Pascaris, Alysia, Leslie Reed Shields, and Jessica Wolf, "The Work and Recovery Project: Changing Organizational Culture and Practice in New York

City Outpatient Services," *Psychiatric Rehabilitation Journal*, Vol. 32, No. 1, Summer 2008, pp. 47–54.

390. Pater, Robert, "Cultural Leadership Raising the Level: Part 1," *Professional Safety*, Vol. 57, No. 3, March, 2012, pp. 28–30.
391. Pater, Robert, and Christine Remmo, "Personal Responsibility for Safety," *Professional Safety*, Vol. 57, No. 9, September 2012, pp. 26–29.
392. Paterson, B., I. McIntosh, D. Wilkinson, S. McComish, and I. Smith, "Corrupted Cultures in Mental Health Inpatient Settings. Is Restraint Reduction the Answer?" *Journal of Psychiatric and Mental Health Nursing*, Vol. 20, No. 3, April 2013, pp. 228–235.
393. Pati, Susmita, Josef Reum, Emily Conant, Lucy Wolf Tuton, M. Patricia Scott, Stephanie Abbuhl, and Jeane Ann Grisso, "Tradition Meets Innovation: Transforming Academic Medical Culture at the University of Pennsylvania's Perelman School of Medicine," *Academic Medicine*, Vol. 88, No. 4, April 2013, pp. 461–464.
394. Paul, Christopher, and Isaac R. Porche, "Toward a U.S. Army Cyber Security Culture," *International Journal of Cyber Warfare and Terrorism*, Vol. 1, No. 3, 2011, pp. 70–80.
395. Paulsen, Neil, Victor J. Callan, Tim A. Grice, David Rooney, Cindy Gallois, Elizabeth Jones, Nerina L. Jimmieson, and Prashant Bordia, "Job Uncertainty and Personal Control During Downsizing: A Comparison of Survivors and Victims," *Human Relations*, Vol. 58, No. 4, April 2005, pp. 463–496.
396. Pawar, M., "Creating & Sustaining a Blame-Free Culture: A Foundation for Process Improvement," *Physician Executive*, Vol. 33, No. 4, July–August 2007, pp. 12–14, 16–19.
397. Pennington, Randy G., "Change Performance to Change the Culture," *Industrial and Commercial Training*, Vol. 35, No. 6, 2003, pp. 251–255.
398. ———, "Yes, But How? Nine Tips for Building a Culture Focused on Results, Relationships, and Accountability," *Industrial and Commercial Training*, Vol. 41, No. 3, 2009, pp. 146–150.
399. Peters, Susan, "Inclusive Education in Accelerated and Professional Development Schools: A Case-Based Study of Two School Reform Efforts in the USA," *International Journal of Inclusive Education*, Vol. 6, No. 4, 2002, pp. 287–308.
400. Peterson, Dane K., "Deviant Workplace Behavior and the Organization's Ethical Climate," *Journal of Business and Psychology*, Vol. 17, No. 1, Fall 2002, pp. 47–61.
401. ———, "The Relationship Between Unethical Behavior and the Dimensions of the Ethical Climate Questionnaire," *Journal of Business Ethics*, Vol. 41, No. 4, December 2002, pp. 313–326.

402. Peterson, Michael, and John F. Wilson, "The Culture-Work-Health Model and Work Stress," *American Journal of Health Behavior*, Vol. 26, No. 1, January–February 2002, pp. 16–24.
403. Phelan, Michael W., "Cultural Revitalization Movements in Organization Change Management," *Journal of Change Management,* Vol. 5, No. 1, 2005, pp. 47–56.
404. Phillips, Frank S., and Andrew N. Garman, "Barriers to Entrepreneurship in Healthcare Organizations," *Journal of Health and Human Services Administration*, Vol. 28, No. 4, Spring 2006, pp. 472–484.
405. Phipps, Simone T. A., Leon C. Prieto, and Satish Verma, "Holding the Helm: Exploring the Influence of Transformational Leadership on Group Creativity, and the Moderating Role of Organizational Learning Culture," *Journal of Organizational Culture, Communications & Conflict*, Vol. 16, No. 2, June 2012, pp. 135–146.
406. Pleban, Robert J., Marisa L. Miller, E. Daly Vaughn, David R. James, Richard L. Wampler, and Paul N. Blankenbeckler, *Impact of the Phase II Infantry Advanced Leader Course (ALC)*, Fort Belvoir, Va.: U.S. Army Research Institute for the Behavioral and Social Sciences, 2012.
407. Poghosyan, Lusine, Angela Nannini, and Sean Clarke, "Organizational Climate in Primary Care Settings: Implications for Nurse Practitioner Practice," *Journal of the American Association of Nurse Practitioners*, Vol. 25, No. 3, March 2013, pp. 134–140.
408. Pololi, Linda H., Janet T. Civian, Robert T. Brennan, Andrea L. Dottolo, and Edward Krupat, "Experiencing the Culture of Academic Medicine: Gender Matters, a National Study," *Journal of General Internal Medicine*, Vol. 28, No. 2, February 2013, pp. 201–207.
409. Prati, L. Melita, Amy McMillan-Capehart, and Joy H. Karriker, "Affecting Organizational Identity: A Manager's Influence," *Journal of Leadership & Organizational Studies*, Vol. 15, No. 4, May, 2009, pp. 404–415.
410. Preskill, Hallie, and Shanelle Boyle, "A Multidisciplinary Model of Evaluation Capacity Building," *American Journal of Evaluation*, Vol. 29, No. 4, December 2008, pp. 443–459.
411. Pronovost, Peter J., Sean M. Berenholtz, Christine A. Goeschel, Dale M. Needham, J. Bryan Sexton, David A. Thompson, Lisa H. Lubomski, Jill A. Marsteller, Martin A. Makary, and Elizabeth Hunt, "Creating High Reliability in Health Care Organizations," *Health Services Research*, Vol. 41, No. 4, Part 2, August 2006, pp. 1599–1617.
412. Rai, Rajnish Kumar, "Knowledge Management and Organizational Culture: A Theoretical Integrative Framework," *Journal of Knowledge Management*, Vol. 15, No. 5, 2011, pp. 779–801.

413. Ramakrishnan, Sreekanth, "Vital Missing Link in Organizational Transformation," *Industrial Management*, Vol. 55, No. 1, January/February 2013, p. 8.
414. Rampersad, Hubert K., "The Way to a High-Performance Culture with the Total Performance Scorecard," *Strategic Change*, Vol. 17, No. 1–2, 2008, pp. 43–55.
415. Rees, Richard T., "The Role of HR in Organizational Development and Innovation," *Employment Relations Today*, Vol. 33, No. 4, 2007, pp. 29–35.
416. Richardson, John B., *Real Leadership and the US Army: Overcoming a Failure of Imagination to Conduct Adaptive Work*, Carlisle, Pa.: U.S. Army War College, 2011.
417. Riolli-Saltzman, Laura, and Fred Luthans, "After the Bubble Burst: How Small High-Tech Firms Can Keep in Front of the Wave," *Academy of Management Executive*, Vol. 15, No. 3, August 2001, pp. 114–124.
418. Robbins, Donijo, "Comments on 'Getting to the Roots of Change: Performance Management and Organizational Culture,'" *Public Performance & Management Review*, Vol. 31, No. 4, June 2008, pp. 654–657.
419. Roberts, Russ, and Paul Hirsch, "Evolution and Revolution in the Twenty-First Century: Rules for Organizations and Managing Human Resources," *Human Resource Management*, Vol. 44, No. 2, Summer 2005, pp. 171–176.
420. Robertson, Ed, "Placing Leaders at the Heart of Organizational Communication," *Strategic Communication Management*, Vol. 9, No. 5, 2005, pp. 34–37.
421. Roman, Christopher, "The Cultural Sources of Acquisition Risk," *Defense AT&L Magazine*, Vol. 34, No. 6, November–December 2005, pp. 15–17.
422. Romero, Nuria Lloret, "Outsourcing as a Change Management Tool in Libraries and Documentation Centers," *Bottom Line: Managing Library Finances*, Vol. 24, No. 1, 2011, pp. 73–79.
423. Rowland, Wade, "Reflections on Metaphor and Identity in the Cyber-Corporation," *Journal of Business Ethics*, Vol. 90, No. 1, November 2009, pp. 15–28.
424. Ruchlin, Hirsch S., Nicole L. Dubbs, Mark A. Callahan, and Michael J. Fosina, "The Role of Leadership in Instilling a Culture of Safety: Lessons from the Literature," *Journal of Healthcare Management*, Vol. 49, No. 1, January–February 2004, pp. 47–58.
425. Ruvolo, Catherine M., "The Organizational Culture of Diversity: An Assessment of West Point's Faculty," *Consulting Psychology Journal: Practice and Research*, Vol. 59, No. 1, March 2007, pp. 54–67.
426. Samli, A. Coskun, "Surviving in Chaotic Modern Markets: Strategic Considerations in Turbulent Times," *Journal of Marketing Theory and Practice*, Vol. 14, No. 4, Fall 2006, pp. 315–322.
427. Sammer, Christine E., Kristine Lykens, Karan P. Singh, Douglas A. Mains, and Nuha A. Lackan, "What is Patient Safety Culture? A Review of the Literature," *Journal of Nursing Scholarship*, Vol. 42, No. 2, 2010, pp. 156–165.

428. Sathe, Vijay, and E. Jane Davidson, "Toward a New Conceptualization of Culture Change," in Neal M. Ashkanasy, Celeste P. E. Wilderom, and Mark F. Peterson, eds., *Handbook of Organizational Culture and Climate*, Thousand Oaks, Calif.: Sage Publications, 2000, pp. 117–129.
429. Sauser, William I., Jr., "Empowering Leaders to Craft Organizational Cultures of Character: Conceptual Framework and Examples," *Journal of Leadership, Accountability & Ethics*, Vol. 10, No. 1, 2013, pp. 14–27.
430. Savych, Bogdan, *Toward Incentives for Military Transformation: A Review of Economic Models of Compensation,* Santa Monica, Calif.: RAND Corporation, TR-194-OSD, 2005.
431. Sawa, Ben, and Sonia Swift, "Developing High-Performing Organizations: Keys to Recruiting, Retaining, and Developing People Who Make the Difference," *Leadership and Management in Engineering*, Vol. 13, No. 2, 2013, pp. 96–100.
432. Schein, Edgar H., "Organizational Culture," *American Psychologist*, Vol. 45, No. 2, 1990, pp. 109–119.
433. Schelly, Chelsea, Jennifer E. Cross, William S. Franzen, Pete Hall, and Stu Reeve, "Reducing Energy Consumption and Creating a Conservation Culture in Organizations: A Case Study of One Public School District," *Environment and Behavior*, Vol. 43, No. 3, May 2011, pp. 316–343.
434. Schlager, Melinda D., "An Assessment of Parole Officer and Administrator Attitudes on Organizational Culture and Parole Supervision in a Northeastern State," *Journal of Offender Rehabilitation*, Vol. 47, No. 3, 2008, pp. 271–289.
435. Schlosser, Melanie, "OSUL2013: Fostering Organizational Change Through a Grassroots Planning Process," *College & Research Libraries*, Vol. 72, No. 2, March 2011,pp. 152–165.
436. Schluter, Jessica, Sarah Winch, Kerri Holzhauser, and Amanda Henderson, "Nurses' Moral Sensitivity and Hospital Ethical Climate: A Literature Review," *Nursing Ethics*, Vol. 15, No. 3, May 2008, pp. 304–321.
437. Schneider, Benjamin, Mark G. Ehrhart, and William H. Macey, "Perspectives on Organizational Climate and Culture," in Sheldon Zedeck, ed., *APA Handbook of Industrial and Organizational Psychology*, Washington, D.C.: American Psychological Association, 2011.
438. ———, "Organizational Climate and Culture," *Annual Review of Psychology*, Vol. 64, 2013, pp. 361–388.
439. Schneider, Benjamin, Harold W. Goldstein, and D. Brent Smith, "The ASA Framework: An Update," *Personnel Psychology*, Vol. 48, 1995, pp. 747–773.
440. Schraeder, Mike, and Dennis R. Self, "Enhancing the Success of Mergers and Acquisitions: An Organizational Culture Perspective," *Management Decision*, Vol. 41, No. 5, 2003, pp. 511–522.
441. Schraeder, Mike, Rachel S. Tears, and Mark H. Jordan, "Organizational Culture in Public Sector Organizations: Promoting Change Through Training and Lead-

ing by Example," *Leadership & Organization Development Journal*, Vol. 26, No. 6, 2005, pp. 492–502.

442. Schroeder, Peter J., "Changing Team Culture: The Perspectives of Ten Successful Head Coaches," *Journal of Sport Behavior*, Vol. 33, No. 1, 2010, pp. 63–88.
443. Schroeder, Peter J., and Jay Paredes Scribner, "'To Honor and Glorify God': The Role of Religion in One Intercollegiate Athletics Culture," *Sport Education and Society*, Vol. 11, No. 1, February 2006, pp. 39–54.
444. Schwartz, Richard W., and Kenneth H. Cohn, "The Necessity for Physician Involvement in Strategic Planning in Healthcare Organizations," *American Journal of Surgery*, Vol. 184, No. 3, September 2002, pp. 269–278.
445. Scott, Tim, Russell Mannion, Huw Davies, and Martin Marshall, "The Quantitative Measurement of Organizational Culture in Health Care: A Review of the Available Instruments," *Health Services Research*, Vol. 38, No. 3, June 2003, pp. 923–945.
446. ———, "Implementing Culture Change in Health Care: Theory and Practice," *International Journal for Quality in Health Care*, Vol. 15, No. 2, April 2003, pp. 111–118.
447. Scott-Findlay, Shannon, and Karen Golden-Biddle, "Understanding How Organizational Culture Shapes Research Use," *Journal of Nursing Administration*, Vol. 35, No. 7–8, July–August 2005, pp. 359–365.
448. Sekerka, Leslie E., "Organizational Ethics Education and Training: A Review of Best Practices and Their Application," *International Journal of Training and Development*, Vol. 13, No. 2, June 2009, pp. 77–95.
449. Seltzer, Trent, Elizabeth Gardner, Shannon Bichard, and Coy Callison, "PR in the ER: Managing Internal Organization-Public Relationships in a Hospital Emergency Department," *Public Relations Review*, Vol. 38, No. 1, March 2012, pp. 128–136.
450. Shackelton, Rebecca, Carol Link, Lisa Marceau, and John McKinlay, "Does the Culture of a Medical Practice Affect the Clinical Management of Diabetes by Primary Care Providers?" *Journal of Health Services Research & Policy*, Vol. 14, No. 2, April 2009, pp. 96–103.
451. Shapiro, Mary, Cynthia Ingols, Regina O'Neill, and Stacy Blake-Beard, "Making Sense of Women as Career Self-Agents: Implications for Human Resource Development," *Human Resource Development Quarterly*, Vol. 20, No. 4, Winter 2009, pp. 477–501.
452. Sharoni, Gil, Aharon Tziner, Erich C. Fein, Tamar Shultz, Keren Shaul, and Lian Zilberman, "Organizational Citizenship Behavior and Turnover Intentions: Do Organizational Culture and Justice Moderate Their Relationship?" *Journal of Applied Social Psychology*, Vol. 42, 2012, pp. E267–E294.

453. Shearer, Corrinne S., David S. Hames, and Janet B. Runge, "How CEOs Influence Organizational Culture Following Acquisitions," *Leadership & Organization Development Journal*, Vol. 22, No. 3, 2001, pp. 105–113.
454. Sherer, Jennifer Zoltners, and James Spillane, "Constancy and Change in Work Practice in Schools: The Role of Organizational Routines," *Teachers College Record*, Vol. 113,No. 3, March 2011, pp. 611–657.
455. Shivers-Blackwell, Sheryl, "The Influence of Perceptions of Organizational Structure & Culture on Leadership Role Requirements: The Moderating Impact of Locus of Control & Self-Monitoring," *Journal of Leadership & Organizational Studies*, Vol. 12, No. 4, Summer 2006, pp. 27–49.
456. Shollen, S. Lynn, Carole J. Bland, Deborah A. Finstad, and Anne L. Taylor, "Organizational Climate and Family Life: How These Factors Affect the Status of Women Faculty at One Medical School," *Academic Medicine*, Vol. 84, No. 1, January 2009, pp. 87–94.
457. Shook, John, "How to Change a Culture: Lessons from NUMMI," *MIT Sloan Management Review*, Vol. 51, No. 2, Winter 2010, pp. 63–68.
458. Sierpina, Victor, Robert Bulik, Constance Baldwin, Moshe Frenkel, Susie Gerik, Dierdra Walters, and Ann Frye, "Creating Sustainable Curricular Change: Lessons Learned from an Alternative Therapies Educational Initiative," *Academic Medicine*, Vol. 82, No. 4, April 2007, pp. 341–350.
459. Simpson, D. Dwayne, "Organizational Readiness for Stage-Based Dynamics of Innovation Implementation," *Research on Social Work Practice*, Vol. 19, No. 5, September 2009, pp. 541–551.
460. Simpson, D. Dwayne, George W. Joe, and Grace A. Rowan-Szal, "Linking the Elements of Change: Program and Client Responses to Innovation," *Journal of Substance Abuse Treatment*, Vol. 33, No. 2, September 2007, pp. 201–209.
461. Sims, Ronald R., and Johannes Brinkman, "Leaders as Moral Role Models: The Case of John Gutfreund at Salomon Brothers," *Journal of Business Ethics*, Vol. 35, No. 4, February 2002, pp. 327–339.
462. Singer, Sara J., and Timothy J. Vogus, "Reducing Hospital Errors: Interventions That Build Safety Culture," *Annual Review of Public Health*, Vol. 34, 2013, pp. 373–396.
463. Smart, John C., "Organizational Effectiveness of 2-Year Colleges: The Centrality of Cultural and Leadership Complexity," *Research in Higher Education*, Vol. 44, No. 6, December 2003, pp. 673–703.
464. Smith, Brenda D., and Irene T. Manfredo, "Frontline Counselors in Organizational Contexts: A Study of Treatment Practices in Community Settings," *Journal of Substance Abuse Treatment*, Vol. 41, No. 2, September 2011, pp. 124–136.
465. Smith, Brien N., Ray V. Montagno, and Tatiana N. Kuzmenko, "Transformational and Servant Leadership: Content and Contextual Comparisons," *Journal of Leadership & Organizational Studies*, Vol. 10, No. 4, Spring 2004, pp. 80–91.

466. Smith, Diana McLain, "Changing Culture Change," *Reflections*, Vol. 12, No. 1, 2012, pp. 1–13.
467. Smith, Rich, and Kittie W. Watson, "The A.R.T. of Diversity: Transforming Stereotypes," *OD Practitioner*, Vol. 41, No. 4, 2009, pp. 25–30.
468. Smith, Teresa M., *Instilling a Culture of Accountability at the Department of Homeland Security (DHS): Leveraging the Government Performance and Results Modernization Act of 2010*, Monterey, Calif.: Naval Postgraduate School, 2013.
469. Snell, Roy, "What Has Changed Over the Last 10 Years in Compliance?" *Journal of Health Care Compliance*, Vol. 13, No. 3, 2011, p. 45.
470. Soeters, Joseph L., "Culture in Uniformed Organizations," in Neal M. Ashkanasy, Celeste P. M. Wilderom, and Mark F. Peterson, eds., *Handbook of Organizational Culture and Climate*, Thousand Oaks, Calif.: Sage Publications, 2000.
471. Spath, Robin, Virginia C. Strand, and Stephanie Bosco-Ruggiero, "What Child Welfare Staff Say About Organizational Culture," *Child Welfare*, Vol. 92, No. 1, 2013, pp. 9–31.
472. Springer, Pamela J., Cynthia M. Clark, Pamela Strohfus, and Marcia Belcheir, "Using Transformational Change to Improve Organizational Culture and Climate in a School of Nursing," *Journal of Nursing Education*, Vol. 51, No. 2, February 2012, pp. 80–87.
473. Stecher, Brian M., Frank Camm, Cheryl L. Damberg, Laura S. Hamilton, Kathleen J. Mullen, Christopher Nelson, Paul Sorensen, Martin Wachs, Allison Yoh, Gail L. Zellman, and Kristin J. Leuschner, *Toward a Culture of Consequences: Improving Performance-Based Accountability for Public Services*, Santa Monica, Calif.: RAND Corporation, MG-1019, 2010.
474. Steele, William, and Robert Walters, Jr., "Training and Developing Army Leaders," *Military Review: The Professional Journal of the US Army*, Vol. 81, No. 4, July–August 2001, pp. 2–9.
475. Stern, Marc F., Robert B. Greifinger, and Jeff Mellow, "Patient Safety: Moving the Bar in Prison Health Care Standards," *American Journal of Public Health*, Vol. 100, No. 11, November 2010, pp. 2103–2110.
476. Stevens, Betsy, "Corporate Ethical Codes as Strategic Documents: An Analysis of Success and Failure," *Electronic Journal of Business Ethics and Organization Studies*, Vol. 14, No. 2, 2009, pp. 14–20.
477. Stoica, Michael, Jianwen Liao, and Harold Welsch, "Organizational Culture and Patterns of Information Processing: The Case of Small and Medium-Sized Enterprises," *Journal of Developmental Entrepreneurship*, Vol. 9, No. 3, 2004, pp. 251–266.
478. Stone, Patricia W., Cathy Mooney-Kane, Elaine L. Larson, Diane K. Pastor, Jack Zwanziger, and Andrew W. Dick, "Nurse Working Conditions, Organizational

Climate, and Intent to Leave in ICUs: An Instrumental Variable Approach," *Health Services Research*, Vol. 42, No. 3, Part 1, June 2007, pp. 1085–1104.

479. Stone, Patricia W., Monika Pogorzelska, Denise Graham, Haomiao Jia, Mayuko Uchida, and Elaine L. Larson, "California Hospitals' Response to State and Federal Policies Related to Health Care-Associated Infections," *Policy, Politics, & Nursing Practice*, Vol. 12, No. 2, May 2011, pp. 73–81.

480. Strickland, Ruth Ann, "The Hierarchy of Ethical Values in Nonprofit Organizations," *Public Integrity*, Vol. 10, No. 3, Summer 2008, pp. 233–251.

481. Taxman, Faye S., Karen L. Cropsey, Gerald Melnick, and Matthew L. Perdoni, "COD Services in Community Correctional Settings: An Examination of Organizational Factors That Affect Service Delivery," *Behavioral Sciences & the Law*, Vol. 26, No. 4, 2008, pp. 435–455.

482. Taxman, Faye S., and Jill A. Gordon, "Do Fairness and Equity Matter? An Examination of Organizational Justice Among Correctional Officers in Adult Prisons," *Criminal Justice and Behavior*, Vol. 36, No. 7, July 2009, pp. 695–711.

483. Taxman, Faye S., Craig Henderson, Doug Young, and Jill Farrell, "The Impact of Training Interventions on Organizational Readiness to Support Innovations in Juvenile Justice Offices," *Administration and Policy in Mental Health and Mental Health Services Research*, Vol. 41, No. 2, March 2014, pp. 177–188.

484. Taylor, George, "Implementing and Maintaining a Knowledge Sharing Culture via Knowledge Management Teams: A Shared Leadership Approach," *Journal of Organizational Culture, Communications & Conflict*, Vol. 17, No. 1, 2013.

485. Teixeira, Eduardo de Oliveira, and William B. Werther, "Resilience: Continuous Renewal of Competitive Advantages," *Business Horizons*, Vol. 56, No. 3, May–June 2013, pp. 333–342.

486. Teleki, Stephanie S., Cheryl L. Damberg, Melony E. Sorbero, Rebecca N. Shaw, Lily A. Bradley, Denise D. Quigley, Allen M. Fremont, and Donna O. Farley, "Training a Patient Safety Work Force: The Patient Safety Improvement Corps," *Health Services Research*, Vol. 44, No. 2, Pt. 2, April 2009, pp. 701–716.

487. Tenbrunsel, Ann E., Kristin Smith-Crowe, and Elizabeth E. Umphress, "Building Houses on Rocks: The Role of the Ethical Infrastructure in Organizations," *Social Justice Research*, Vol. 16, No. 3, September 2003, pp. 285–307.

488. Terriff, Terry, "Warriors and Innovators: Military Change and Organizational Culture in the US Marine Corps," *Defence Studies*, Vol. 6, No. 2, 2006, pp. 215–247.

489. Terry, Paul E., "The Mutualism of Culture and Engagement," *American Journal of Health Promotion*, Vol. 26, No. 6, 2012, pp. TAHP-1–TAHP-12.

490. The Military Leadership Diversity Commission, *From Representation to Inclusion: Diversity Leadership for the 21st-Century Military*, Arlington, Va.: The Military Leadership Diversity Commission, 2011.

491. Thoroughgood, Christian N., Samuel T. Hunter, and Katina B. Sawyer, "Bad Apples, Bad Barrels, and Broken Followers? An Empirical Examination of Contextual Influences on Follower Perceptions and Reactions to Aversive Leadership," *Journal of Business Ethics*, Vol. 100, No. 4, June, 2011, pp. 647–672.
492. Tobias, Lester L., "The Thriving Person and the Thriving Organization Parallels and Linkages," *Consulting Psychology Journal: Practice and Research*, Vol. 56, No. 1, 2004, pp. 3–9.
493. Tobin, Timothy J., Ralph O. Muller, and Lauren M. Turner, "Organizational Learning and Climate as Predictors of Self-Efficacy," *Social Psychology of Education*, Vol. 9, No. 3, August 2006, pp. 301–319.
494. Tran, Ny Mia, and Bryan L. Dawson, "Reevaluating the Concept of Diversity Management: Considerations for Diversity Trainers and Educators," *Academy of Management Learning & Education*, Vol. 7, No. 3, 2008, pp. 406–417.
495. Tran, Thuhang, "A Conceptual Model of Learning Culture and Innovation Schema," *Competitiveness Review*, Vol. 18, No. 3, 2008, pp. 287–299.
496. Treverton, Gregory F., *Reorganizing U.S. Domestic Intelligence: Assessing the Options*, Santa Monica, Calif.: RAND Corporation, MG-767-DHS, 2008.
497. Trevino, Linda Klebe, and Michael E. Brown, "Managing to Be Ethical: Debunking Five Business Ethics Myths," *Academy of Management Executive*, Vol. 18, No. 2, 2004, pp. 69–81.
498. Trompenaars, Fons, and Peter Woolliams, "A New Framework for Managing Change Across Cultures," *Journal of Change Management*, Vol. 3, No. 4, 2003, pp. 361–375.
499. Turnbeaugh, Treasa M., "Improving Business Outcomes," *Professional Safety*, Vol. 55, No. 3, March 2010, pp. 41–49.
500. Turnberg, Wayne, and William Daniell, "Evaluation of a Healthcare Safety Climate Measurement Tool," *Journal of Safety Research*, Vol. 39, No. 6, 2008, pp. 563–568.
501. Turnipseed, Patricia H., and David L. Turnipseed, "Testing the Proposed Linkage Between Organizational Citizenship Behaviours and an Innovative Organizational Climate," *Creativity and Innovation Management*, Vol. 22, No. 2, June 2013, pp. 209–216.
502. Turregano, Clemson G., and Thomas G. Gaffney, "Creating a Shared Leadership Culture Through Multilevel Development," *Public Manager*, Vol. 41, No. 3, September 2012, pp. 19–21.
503. Tyler, Tom R., Patrick E. Callahan, and Jeffrey Frost, "Armed, and Dangerous (?): Motivating Rule Adherence Among Agents of Social Control," *Law & Society Review*, Vol. 41, No. 2, 2007, pp. 457–492.
504. Ulrich, Dave, Justin Allen, Norm Smallwood, Wayne Brockbank, and Jon Younger, "Building Culture from the Outside in," *Strategic HR Review*, Vol. 8, No. 6, 2009, pp. 20–27.

505. Uniformed Services University, "Uniformed Services University Seven Strategic Goals," *Uniformed Services University of the Health Sciences Journal*, 2001.
506. Valentine, Dawn B., "Maintaining Organization Culture Through Leadership Succession Planning," *Franklin Business & Law Journal*, No. 4, June 2011, p. 103.
507. Vales, Elizabeth, "Employees CAN Make a Difference! Involving Employees in Change at Allstate Insurance," *Organization Development Journal*, Vol. 25, No. 4, 2007, pp. P27–P31.
508. Vallejo, Manuel Carlos, "A Model to Study the Organizational Culture of the Family Firm," *Small Business Economics*, Vol. 36, No. 1, January 2011, pp. 47–64.
509. Van Fleet, David D., and Ricky W. Griffin, "Dysfunctional Organization Culture: The Role of Leadership in Motivating Dysfunctional Work Behaviors," *Journal of Managerial Psychology*, Vol. 21, No. 8, 2006, pp. 698–708.
510. Van Niekerk, J. F., and R. Von Solms, "Information Security Culture: A Management Perspective," *Computers & Security*, Vol. 29, No. 4, June 2010, pp. 476–486.
511. Vance, Charles, Deone Zell, and Kevin Groves, "Considering Individual Linear/Nonlinear Thinking Style and Innovative Corporate Culture," *International Journal of Organizational Analysis*, Vol. 16, No. 4, 2008, pp. 232–248.
512. VanSandt, Craig V., and Christopher P. Neck, "Bridging Ethics and Self Leadership: Overcoming Ethical Discrepancies Between Employee and Organizational Standards," *Journal of Business Ethics*, Vol. 43, No. 4, April 2003, pp. 363–387.
513. Vest, Hugh S., *Employee Warriors and the Future of the American Fighting Force: Fairchild Paper*, Maxwell Air Force Base, Ala.: Air University, 2012.
514. Voelpel, Sven C., Marius Leibold, and Christoph K. Streb, "The Innovation Meme: Managing Innovation Replicators for Organizational Fitness," *Journal of Change Management*, Vol. 5, No. 1, March 2005, pp. 57–69.
515. Wagner, Laura M., Shawna M. McDonald, and Nicholas G. Castle, "Relationship Between Nursing Home Safety Culture and Joint Commission Accreditation," *The Joint Commission Journal on Quality and Patient Safety*, Vol. 38, No. 5, May, 2012, pp. 207–215.
516. Walker, Nefertiti A., and Melanie L. Sartore-Baldwin, "Hegemonic Masculinity and the Institutionalized Bias Toward Women in Men's Collegiate Basketball: What Do Men Think?" *Journal of Sport Management*, Vol. 27, No. 4, July 2013, pp. 303–315.
517. Walker-Fraser, Alison, "An HR Perspective on Executive Coaching for Organisational Learning," *International Journal of Evidence Based Coaching and Mentoring*, Vol. 9, No. 2, August, 2011, pp. 67–79.
518. Wallen, Gwyneth R., Sandra A. Mitchell, Bernadette Melnyk, Ellen Fineout-Overholt, Claiborne Miller-Davis, Janice Yates, and Clare Hastings, "Implementing Evidence-Based Practice: Effectiveness of a Structured Multifac-

eted Mentorship Programme," *Journal of Advanced Nursing*, Vol. 66, No. 12, December 2010, pp. 2761–2771.

519. Wang, Margaret C., Jenny K. Hyun, Michael Harrison, Stephen M. Shortell, and Irene Fraser, "Redesigning Health Systems for Quality: Lessons from Emerging Practices," *The Joint Commission Journal on Quality and Patient Safety*, Vol. 32, No. 11, November 2006, pp. 599–611.
520. Wang, Wei, Lisa Saldana, C. Hendricks Brown, and Patricia Chamberlain, "Factors that Influenced County System Leaders to Implement an Evidence-Based Program: A Baseline Survey Within a Randomized Controlled Trial," *Implementation Science*, Vol. 5, October 6, 2010.
521. Warner, Christopher H., and George Appenzeller, "Engaged Leadership: Linking the Professional Ethic and Battlefield Behaviors," *Military Review*, Vol. 91, No. 5, 2011, pp. 61–69.
522. Warren, Danielle E., Joseph P. Gaspar, and William S. Laufer, "Is Formal Ethics Training Merely Cosmetic? A Study of Ethics Training and Ethical Organizational Culture," *Business Ethics Quarterly*, Vol. 24, No. 1, January 2014, pp. 85–117.
523. Warren, Nicholas, Michael Hodgson, Thomas Craig, Sue Dyrenforth, Jonathan Perlin, Frances Murphy, and Administration Veterans Health, "Employee Working Conditions and Healthcare System Performance: The Veterans Health Administration Experience," *Journal of Occupational & Environmental Medicine*, Vol. 49, No. 4, April 2007, pp. 417–429.
524. Waters, V. Lynn, "Cultivate Corporate Culture and Diversity," *Nursing Management*, Vol. 35, No. 1, January 2004, pp. 36–37.
525. Waugh, William L., and Gregory Streib, "Collaboration and Leadership for Effective Emergency Management," *Public Administration Review*, Vol. 66, December 2006, pp. 131–140.
526. Weeks, William A., Terry W. Loe, Lawrence B. Chonko, and Kirk Wakefield, "The Effect of Perceived Ethical Climate on the Search for Sales Force Excellence," *Journal of Personal Selling & Sales Management*, Vol. 24, No. 3, Summer 2004, pp. 199–214.
527. Wehrenberg, Stephen, "The Coast Guard Charts a Course for Enterprise Change Management," *Global Business and Organizational Excellence*, Vol. 29, No. 1, November/December 2009, pp. 17–31.
528. Weiner, Bryan J., Charles M. Belden, Dawn M. Bergmire, and Matthew Johnston, "The Meaning and Measurement of Implementation Climate," *Implementation Science*, Vol. 6, 2011, p. 78.
529. Whitman, Daniel S., Suzette Caleo, Nichelle C. Carpenter, Margaret T. Horner, and Jeremy B. Bernerth, "Fairness at the Collective Level: A Meta-Analytic Examination of the Consequences and Boundary Conditions of Organizational Justice Climate," *Journal of Applied Psychology*, Vol. 97, No. 4, July 2012, pp. 776–791.

530. Wilkinson, Brett, Vicky Arnold, and Steve G. Sutton, "Understanding the Socialization Strategies of the Major Accountancy Firms," *Accounting and the Public Interest*, Vol. 3, No. 1, December, 2003, pp. 58–79.
531. Williams, Nathaniel J., and Charles Glisson, "Reducing Turnover Is Not Enough: The Need for Proficient Organizational Cultures to Support Positive Youth Outcomes in Child Welfare," *Children and Youth Services Review*, Vol. 35, No. 11, November 2013, pp. 1871–1877.
532. Williams, Stephanie M., and Melanie L. Hatch, "Influences of School Superintendents' Servant Leadership Practices to Length of Tenure," *Journal of Organizational Learning and Leadership*, Vol. 10, No. 2, Fall and Winter 2012, pp. 36–58.
533. Williamsen, Mike, "Near-Miss Reporting," *Professional Safety*, May 2013, pp. 46–50.
534. Wilson, Deleise, Richard W. Redman, AkkeNeel Talsma, and Michelle Aebersold, "Differences in Perceptions of Patient Safety Culture Between Charge and Noncharge Nurses: Implications for Effectiveness Outcomes Research," *Nursing Research and Practice*, 2012, pp. 1–7.
535. Wolf, David A. Patterson Silver (Adelv unegv Waya), Catherine N. Dulmus, and Eugene Maguin, "Is Openness to Using Empirically Supported Treatments Related to Organizational Culture and Climate?" *Journal of Social Service Research*, Vol. 39, No. 4, 2013, pp. 562–571.
536. Wolf, Jessica, Lyn H. Lawrence, Patrick M. Ryan, and Michael A. Hoge, "Emerging Practices in Employment of Persons in Recovery in the Mental Health Workforce," *American Journal of Psychiatric Rehabilitation*, Vol. 13, No. 3, 2010, pp. 189–207.
537. Wong, Leonard, Paul Bliese, and Dennis McGurk, "Military Leadership: A Context Specific Review," *Leadership Quarterly*, Vol. 14, No. 6, December 2003, pp. 657–692.
538. Wortzel-Hoffman, Nina, and Sarah Boltizar, "Performance and Development Planning: A Culture Shift Perspective," *Organization Development Journal*, Vol. 25, No. 2, June 2007, pp. P195–P233.
539. Wright, Lisa, "Quality Improvement and Organizational Change Initiatives: An Analysis of the U.S. Army's Warrior Transition Unit (WTU)," *Academy of Strategic Management Journal*, Vol. 12, No. 2, July 2013, pp. 95–111.
540. Wukitsch, Michael, Ryan Simmons, and Mark Hutt, "Rearticulating Values Through Applied Theories at Children's Hospital Colorado," *Advances in Developing Human Resources*, Vol. 15, No. 3, August, 2013, pp. 252–269.
541. Yackel, Edward E., Nancy M. Short, Pul C. Lewis, Sara T. Breckenridge-Sproat, and Barbara S. Turner, "Improving the Adoption of Evidence-Based Practice Among Nurses in Army Outpatient Medical Treatment Facilities," *Military Medicine*, Vol. 178, No. 9, September 2013, pp. 1002–1009.

542. Yaghi, Abdulfattah, "Leadership Values Influencing Decision-Making: An Examination of Nine Islamic, Hindu, and Christian Nonprofit Institutions in the U.S.," *South Asian Journal of Management,* Vol. 15, No. 1, January–March 2008, pp. 24–41.
543. Yang, Baiyin, "Identifying Valid and Reliable Measures for Dimensions of a Learning Culture," *Advances in Developing Human Resources,* Vol. 5, No. 2, May 2003, pp. 152–162.
544. Yauch, Charlene A., and Harold J. Steudel, "Complementary Use of Qualitative and Quantitative Cultural Assessment Methods," *Organizational Research Methods,* Vol. 6, No. 4, October 2003, pp. 465–481.
545. Zazzali, James L., Jeffrey A. Alexander, Stephen M. Shortell, and Lawton R. Burns, "Organizational Culture and Physician Satisfaction with Dimensions of Group Practice," *Health Services Research,* Vol. 42, No. 3, Pt. 1, June 2007, pp. 1150–1176.
546. Zazzali, James L., Cathy Sherbourne, Kimberly E. Hoagwood, Deborah Greene, Michael F. Bigley, and Thomas L. Sexton, "The Adoption and Implementation of an Evidence Based Practice in Child and Family Mental Health Services Organizations: A Pilot Study of Functional Family Therapy in New York State," *Administration and Policy in Mental Health and Mental Health Services Research,* Vol. 35, No. 1–2, March 2008, pp. 38–49.
547. Zilber, Tammar B., "The Relevance of Institutional Theory for the Study of Organizational Culture," *Journal of Management Inquiry,* Vol. 21, No. 1, January 2012, pp. 88–93.
548. Zohar, Dov, and David Hofmann, "Organizational Culture and Climate," in Steve J. Kozlowski, eds.,The Oxford Handbook of Organizational Psychology, New York: Oxford University Press, Vol. 1, 2012, pp. 643–666.
549. Zohar, Dov, and Tal Polachek, "Discourse-Based Intervention for Modifying Supervisory Communication as Leverage for Safety Climate and Performance Improvement: A Randomized Field Study," *Journal of Applied Psychology,* Vol. 99, No. 1, January 2014, pp. 113–124.

APPENDIX C

Summary of Definitions of Culture

Definition[a]	Source	Level	Development	Receptivity
"the shared beliefs and values that are passed on to all within the organization"	Davidson, 2003, as cited in Koutroumanis and Alexakis, 2009	Deep	Top-down	Unclear
"the deep structure of organizations, which is rooted in the values, beliefs, and assumptions held by organizational members"	Denison, 1996	Deep	Unclear	Unclear
"what your employees do when no one is looking. It's a set of values, norms, and unspoken ideas that produces a predictable human response"	Peshawaria, 2009, as cited in Gandossy et al., 2009	Deep	Unclear	Unclear
"deeply rooted traditions, values, beliefs, and sense-of self"	Sopow, 2006, as cited in Heldenbrand and Simms, 2012	Deep	Unclear	Resistant
"a set of assumptions or an interpretative framework that undergirds daily life in an organization or occupation"	Barley, 1983, as cited in Lurie and Riccucci, 2003	Deep	Unclear	Unclear
"the characteristic way and values through which work is done in organizations"	Cabrera and Bonache, 1999, as cited in Riolli-Saltzman and Luthans, 2001	Deep and surface	Unclear	Unclear
"the taken-for-granted values, the underlying assumptions, expectations, collective memories, and definitions present in the organization"	Cameron and Quinn, 1999, as cited in Koutroumanis and Alexakis, 2009	Deep	Unclear	Unclear

Definition[a]	Source	Level	Development	Receptivity
"Pattern of basic assumptions that a given group has invented, discovered or developed in learning to cope with its problems of external adaptation and internal integration, and that have worked well enough to be considered valid, and, therefore, to be taught to new members as the correct way to perceive, think, and feel in relation to those problems."	Schein 1992, as cited in Frontiera, 2010	Deep	Top-down	Open
"the existing ideologies, values, norms and expectations shared by an organization which affects its members and performance"	Valentine, 2011	Deep	Unclear	Unclear
"organizational practices and the consequences of those practices"	Clayton et al. 1997, as cited in Bumstead and Boyce, 2004	Surface	Unclear	Unclear
"a set of cognitions shared by members of a social unit and that are acquired through social learning and a socialization process exposing individuals to a variety of culture-bearing elements, such as the observable activities and interactions, communicated information, and artifacts"	Cooke and Rouseau, 1988, as cited in Jaskyte et al., 2010	Deep and surface	Top-down and bottom-up	Unclear
"the normative beliefs and shared behavioral expectations in an organization or work unit"	Cooke and Szumal,1993, as cited in Glisson, 2002	Deep	Unclear	Unclear
"the hidden curriculum of fundamental value systems, rituals, and routines, initiations and acceptance that forms the fabric of daily life (in schools)"	Corbett, as cited in Ware, 2000: Peters, 2002	Deep	Unclear	Unclear
"a diffusion of the work-a-day world in which ways of doing work become habitual and habits become meaningful"	Crank, 1998, as cited in Kingshott, 2009	Deep and surface	Unclear	Unclear
"compilation of shared meaning in a unique environment and is characterized by the pattern of basic underlying assumptions, espoused values, norms, and artifacts shared by the organizational members"	Cummings and Worley, 2001, as cited in Foote and Ruona, 2008	Deep and surface	Top-down and bottom-up	Unclear
"norms, values, and beliefs, and is reflected by its stories, rituals and rites, symbols, and language"	Daft, 2000, as cited in Zazzali et al., 2007	Deep and surface	Unclear	Unclear
"set of values, guiding beliefs, understandings, and ways of thinking that is shared by members of an organization and taught to new members as correct"	Daft, 2000, as cited in Zazzali et al., 2008	Deep and surface	Top-down and bottom-up	Unclear

Definition[a]	Source	Level	Development	Receptivity
"the underground stream of norms, values, beliefs, traditions and rituals that has built up over time as people work together, solve problems and confront challenges"	Deal and Peterson, 1998, as cited in Arriaza, 2004	Deep	Top-down and bottom-up	Unclear
"the deep structure of organizations, which is rooted in the values, beliefs, and assumptions held by organizational members" and that is "rooted in history, collectively held, and sufficiently complex to resist many attempts at direct manipulation"	Denison, 1996, as cited in Seltzer, et al., 2012	Deep	Top-down and bottom-up	Resistant
"an interlocking set of goals, roles, processes, values, communications practices, attitudes, and assumptions [that] fit together as a mutually reinforcing system and combine to prevent any attempt to change it"	Denning, 2011, as cited in Heckelman, 2013	Deep and surface	Unclear	Resistant
"the pattern of shared values and beliefs that help give the members of an organization meaning, and provide them with the rules for behavior in the organization"	Deshpande and Webster, 1987, as cited in Dosoglu-Guner, 2001	Deep	Unclear	Unclear
"an organization's value system, its collection of guiding principles and is driven by leadership"	Evans and Lindsay, 2008, as cited in Wright, 2013	Deep	Top-down	Open
"means there are people who share a common history in some way, have a common sense of belonging, and are therefore readily able to engage with other people who share these feelings"	Flood, 1996, as cited in Huq, Huq, and Cartwright, 2006	Deep	Unclear	Unclear
"the organizational norms and expectations regarding how people behave and how things are done in an organization"	Glisson and James, 2002, as cited in Aarons and Sawitzky, 2006	Deep	Unclear	Unclear
"the way things are done in an organization or the system's work norms"	Glisson, 2007, as cited in Gregory et al., 2012	Deep and surface	Unclear	Unclear
"the sum of the beliefs and values held in common by those within the organization, serving to formally and informally communicate what is expected"	Gould, 1997, as cited in Kingshott, 2009	Deep	Top-down and bottom-up	Unclear
"the collective behaviors of individuals within that organization"	Handy, 1976, as cited in Ulrich et al., 2009	Deep	Top-down and bottom-up	Open
"software of the mind" or the shared patterns of thought, emotion, and action that distinguish one group of people from other groups"	Hofstede and Hofstede, 2005, as cited in Lyons, 2010	Deep	Unclear	Unclear

Definition[a]	Source	Level	Development	Receptivity
"collective programming of the mind that distinguishes the members of one organization from another"	Hofstede and Hofstede, 2005, pp. 282–283, as cited in Lyons, 2010	Deep	Top-down and bottom-up	Unclear
"the interactive aggregate of common characteristics that influence a human group's response to its environment"	Hofstede, 2001, as cited in Bruhn and Lowrey, 2012	Unclear	Top-down and bottom-up	Unclear
"the shared philosophies, ideologies, values, assumptions, beliefs, expectations, attitudes and norms that knit a community together"	Kilman, Saxton, and Serpa, 1986, as cited in Lurie and Riccucci, 2003	Deep	Unclear	Unclear
"patterned ways of thinking, feeling and reacting, acquired and transmitted by symbols, constituting the distinctive achievements of human groups"	Kluckhohn, 1951, as cited in Bruhn and Lowrey, 2012	Deep and surface	Top-down	Unclear
"the values, beliefs, and expectations of employees, helping to set expectations and shape behaviors of employees"	Lahiry, 1994, as cited in Bell, Quick, and Cycyota., 2002	Deep	Top-down and bottom-up	Unclear
"the assumptions, ideas and beliefs, expressed or reflected in organizational symbols, rituals, and practices that give meaning to the activity of the organization"	Legro, 1995, as cited in Terriff, 2006	Deep and surface	Unclear	Unclear
"set of meanings shared by a group of people"	Louis, 1985, as cited in Frontiera, 2010	Deep	Unclear	Unclear
"an organization's values, beliefs, practices, rituals, and customs"	Marquardt, 2002, as cited in Graham and Nafukho, 2007	Deep and surface	Unclear	Unclear
"a system of shared values (that define what is important) and norms that define appropriate attitudes and behaviors for organizational members"	O'Reilly and Chatman, 1996, as cited in Flores et al., 2012	Deep	Unclear	Unclear
"system of generally and collectively accepted meanings which operate for a certain group on a certain occasion"	Pettigrew, 1979, as cited in Bellot, 2011	Deep	Unclear	Unclear
"The set of important assumptions (often unstated) that members of a community share in common"	Sathe, 1985, as cited in Glisson, 2002	Deep	Unclear	Unclear
"the way we do things around here"	Schein, 1965, 1985, as cited in Hopkins, 2006, Turnbeaug, 2010	Surface	Unclear	Unclear
"basic assumptions and beliefs shared by members of a group or organization, that operate unconsciously"	Schein, 1985, as cited in Sims and Brinkman, 2002	Deep	Unclear	Unclear

Definition[a]	Source	Level	Development	Receptivity
"defined in terms of three elements. Artifacts are the most visible and may include dress, organizational structure, and ceremonies. Espoused beliefs and values are conscious and are evidenced through management practices intended to influence the effectiveness and efficiency of the organization. Underlying assumptions are the unconscious thoughts, expectations, and theories on which artifacts and beliefs/values are founded."	Schein, 2004	Deep and surface	Top-down	Unclear
"the climate and practices that organizations develop around their interaction with people or refer to the espoused values of an organization"	Schein, 1992, as cited in Bruhn and Lowrey, 2012	Deep and surface	Unclear	Unclear
"The sum total of all the shared, taken-for-granted assumptions that a group has learned throughout its history. It is the residue of success."	Schein, 1999, as cited in Buch and Wetzel, 2001	Deep	Top-down and bottom-up	Unclear
"pattern of shared assumptions that people within an organization learn as a group, pass on to new members, and which influences their social interactions"	Schein, 2004, as cited in Lyons, 2010	Deep	Top-down and bottom-up	Unclear
"the system of shared beliefs and values that develops within an organization and guides the behavior of its members"	Schermerhorn, 2005, as cited in Sauser, 2013	Deep	Top-down and bottom-up	Unclear
"the transmitted patterns of values, beliefs and expectations shared by people, including the system of symbols which imparts them to members of the group"	Schreyögg et al., 1995, as cited in Voelpel, Leibold, and Streb, 2005	Deep and surface	Top-down	Unclear
"a normative glue and a set of values, social ideals or beliefs that organization members share"	Siehl and Martin, 1983, as cited in Bellot, 2011	Deep	Unclear	Unclear
"set of contingencies of reinforcement applicable to members of an organization who share a common knowledge"	Skinner, 1971, as cited in Bushardt et al., 2011	Surface	Top-down and bottom-up	Open
the basic assumptions and beliefs that are "shared by members of an organization and that define an organization's view of itself and it's [sic] environment"	Sleutel, 2000, as cited in Narine and Persaud, 2003	Deep	Unclear	Unclear
"social or normative glue that holds an organization together"	Smircich, 1983, as cited in Conceição and Altman, 2011	Deep	Unclear	Unclear
"a 'toolkit'—a collection of rituals, symbols, stories, and worldviews that actors can draw on to construct their action in particular situations"	Swidler, 1986, as cited in Kellogg, 2011	Deep and surface	Unclear	Unclear

Definition[a]	Source	Level	Development	Receptivity
"The norms, values, beliefs, and attitudes embedded in the daily lives of institutional actors give meaning to an organization and, in part, represent what has come to be known as 'organizational culture'"	Tierney, 1988, as cited in Ruvolo, 2007	Deep	Unclear	Unclear
"what personality is to an individual"	Wilson, 1989, as cited in Lurie and Riccucci, 2003	Deep	Unclear	Unclear
"a set of habits and behavior within an organization that are typically exhibited by its members. These are accompanied by typical values, feelings, and beliefs. Together these comprise the 'personality' of an organization."	Balling, 2005	Deep	Unclear	Unclear
"the prevailing implicit and explicit visions, assumptions, rules, norms, and policies of the organization (or subgroup) in which training and psychotherapy take place"	Fauth et al, 2007	Deep and surface	Unclear	Unclear
"the interaction between environmental variables, organizational practices, and the consequences of those practices"	Bumstead and Boyce, 2004	Surface	Unclear	Open
"set of deeply ingrained, taken-for-granted assumptions or beliefs about how people work, about what's important in the workplace, about what's considered 'acceptable' and what's not"	Perlow, 2009, as cited in Gandossy et al., 2009	Deep	Top-down	Unclear
"cohesive system of meanings and symbols, in terms of which social interaction takes place"	Alveeson, 2002, as cited in Bellot, 2011	Deep and surface	Unclear	Unclear
"a human system of closely held beliefs that require certain behaviors and exclude other behaviors. Mostly, it is a set of unwritten rules."	McGuire, Rhodes, and Palus, 2008	Deep	Unclear	Unclear
"patterns of shared meaning in an organization"	Trice and Beyer, 1993, as cited in Robbins, 2008	Deep	Unclear	Unclear
"collections of unspoken rules and traditions and operate 24 hours a day"	Mike and Slocum Jr, 2003	Deep	Unclear	Unclear
"shared perceptions of organizational values and practices within organizational units that both exemplify and reinforce the underlying assumptions and principles of an organization"	Denison, 1990; van den Berg and Wilderom, 2004, as cited in Khoja, 2010	Deep and surface	Unclear	Unclear

Definition[a]	Source	Level	Development	Receptivity
"a system of shared values and beliefs constructed by an organization and by its employees through tangible and intangible cues"	Franklin and Pagan, as cited in Nica, 2013	Deep	Top-down and bottom-up	Unclear
"shared assumptions and values by group members and climate as shared perceptions about organizational conditions"	Lin, 1999, as cited in Wright, 2013	Deep	Top-down and bottom-up	Unclear
"shared values and assumptions of 'how' things should be done (ideal environment)"	Lussier, 2010, as cited in Wright, 2013	Deep	Top-down and bottom-up	Unclear
"manifestations of a process of ideational development located within a context of definite material conditions"	Mills, 1988, as cited in Frontiera, 2010	Deep and surface	Top-down and bottom-up	Unclear
"shared values and expectations by members of the organization"	Hill and Jones, 2001, as cited in Devine et al., 2007	Deep	Top-down and bottom-up	Unclear
"organization's personality which determines how its employees carry out their activities"	Armenakis and Lang, 2014	Deep	Unclear	Unclear
"a system of shared meaning held by its members that distinguishes their organization from other organizations"	Schein, 1996, as cited in Brady and Haley, 2013	Deep	Unclear	Unclear
"the tacit organizational understandings (e.g. assumptions, beliefs and values) that contextualize efforts to make meaning, including internal self-definition"	Hatch and Schultz, 2002	Deep	Unclear	Unclear
"the shared beliefs, perceptions, and expectations of individuals in organizations"	Boan, 2006	Deep	Unclear	Unclear
"an organization's formally and informally expressed understandings of how it is to fulfill its functions and what functions are appropriate for it"	Nielsen, 2010	Deep	Top-down and bottom-up	Unclear
"employees' perceptions and beliefs regarding the organization's typical mode of operation across multiple issues"	Hartmann et al., 2009	Deep	Unclear	Unclear
"the values, attitudes, beliefs, orientations, and underlying assumptions prevalent among people in a society"	Harrison and Huntington, 2000, as cited in Linnean, 2007	Deep	Unclear	Unclear
"organizational culture is holistic, historically determined, and socially constructed, and it involves beliefs and behavior, exists at a variety of levels, and manifests itself in a wide range of features of organizational life"	Detert et al., 2000, as cited in Linnean, 2007	Deep	Top-down and bottom-up	Unclear

Definition[a]	Source	Level	Development	Receptivity
"series of rules and methods which a society or organization has evolved to deal with the regular problems that face it"	Trompenaars and Woolliams, 2003	Deep and surface	Unclear	Unclear
"your organization's DNA—the intangible that guides action based on assumptions, beliefs, and values"	Pennington, 2009	Deep	Unclear	Unclear
"the way an organization functions and gets its business done"	Brown et al., 2003	Surface	Unclear	Unclear
"summarizes collective standards of thinking/attitudes/values/convinces/ norms/ habits of an organization"	Mateiu, Puiu, and Puiu, 2013	Deep	Unclear	Unclear
"the shared values, shared beliefs, and shared rules for acceptable behavior"	Ondeck, 2003	Deep	Unclear	Unclear
"a shared experience by individuals creating a system with meaning, values, and beliefs that influences and shapes individual and group behaviors"	Nold, 2012	Deep	Top-down and bottom-up	Unclear
"the way we do things around here and the manner in which these norms [the 'ways'] and values are communicated"	Deal and Kennedy, 1982, as cited in Burke, 2014	Deep and surface	Unclear	Unclear
"A system of shared, behavioral norms and underlying beliefs and values that shape the way of doing things in an organization"	Verbeke et al., 1998, as cited in Zohar and Hoffman, 2012	Deep	Unclear	Unclear
"Beliefs, ideologies, and values, and the ways these are transmitted through symbols, language, narratives (myths, stories), and practices (rituals and taboos) especially during socialization to the workplace"	Trice and Beyer, 1993, as cited in Schneider et al., 2011	Deep and surface	Top-down and bottom-up	Unclear
"Why it [what goes on in organizations] happens the way it does"	Schneider et al., 2011	Deep	Unclear	Unclear

[a] Definitions were those cited in documents that were part of our literature review. Full citations of those documents are included in Appendix B.

APPENDIX D

SME Panelist Pre-Conference Rating Form

Expert Panelist Pre-Conference Rating Form

We collected and coded **drivers of organizational culture change** based on our literature review. These are shown in the leftmost column of the table below and include drivers that promote organizational change (or in its absence could hinder change). Please rate each driver on the dimensions described in the column headers by selecting a number from 1 to 5 where "5" is highest, or select DK if you don't know on: (1) *alignment* with the Army's mission, and (2) *feasibility*, or whether it is practical to implement the change in the Army; and (3) *reason(s)* for your ratings.

Drivers of Organizational Cultural Change: The Organization or Leadership	Alignment with the Army's Mission	Feasibility of Implementation	Reasons for Ratings (Write In)
Sets goals; uses coherent planning, persistence, and strategic/inspirational/innovative thinking; results oriented	1 ❍ 2 ❍ 3 ❍ 4 ❍ 5 ❍ DK ❍	1 ❍ 2 ❍ 3 ❍ 4 ❍ 5 ❍ DK ❍	
Engages stakeholders, includes diverse perspectives, or develops partnerships	1 ❍ 2 ❍ 3 ❍ 4 ❍ 5 ❍ DK ❍	1 ❍ 2 ❍ 3 ❍ 4 ❍ 5 ❍ DK ❍	
Promotes openness to change/transformation, flexibility, adaptability, optimism, or learning orientation	1 ❍ 2 ❍ 3 ❍ 4 ❍ 5 ❍ DK ❍	1 ❍ 2 ❍ 3 ❍ 4 ❍ 5 ❍ DK ❍	
Systematizes recommendations in day-to-day operations, standards	1 ❍ 2 ❍ 3 ❍ 4 ❍ 5 ❍ DK ❍	1 ❍ 2 ❍ 3 ❍ 4 ❍ 5 ❍ DK ❍	
Develops personnel through training (skills, engagement, etc.), education	1 ❍ 2 ❍ 3 ❍ 4 ❍ 5 ❍ DK ❍	1 ❍ 2 ❍ 3 ❍ 4 ❍ 5 ❍ DK ❍	
Devotes sufficient resources (financial, staffing, tine, etc.) to change efforts	1 ❍ 2 ❍ 3 ❍ 4 ❍ 5 ❍ DK ❍	1 ❍ 2 ❍ 3 ❍ 4 ❍ 5 ❍ DK ❍	
Articulates a clear mission, clear vision/goals, clear expectations/expectation management	1 ❍ 2 ❍ 3 ❍ 4 ❍ 5 ❍ DK ❍	1 ❍ 2 ❍ 3 ❍ 4 ❍ 5 ❍ DK ❍	

Drivers of Organizational Cultural Change: The Organization or Leadership	Alignment with the Army's Mission	Feasibility of Implementation	Reasons for Ratings (Write In)
Uses clear, open, or transparent communication, etc.	1 ❍ 2 ❍ 3 ❍ 4 ❍ 5 ❍ DK ❍	1 ❍ 2 ❍ 3 ❍ 4 ❍ 5 ❍ DK ❍	
Underscores shared responsibilities and accountability	1 ❍ 2 ❍ 3 ❍ 4 ❍ 5 ❍ DK ❍	1 ❍ 2 ❍ 3 ❍ 4 ❍ 5 ❍ DK ❍	
Focuses on trust, empowerment, self-efficacy, etc.	1 ❍ 2 ❍ 3 ❍ 4 ❍ 5 ❍ DK ❍	1 ❍ 2 ❍ 3 ❍ 4 ❍ 5 ❍ DK ❍	
Applies incentives, encouragement, motivation, or rewards	1 ❍ 2 ❍ 3 ❍ 4 ❍ 5 ❍ DK ❍	1 ❍ 2 ❍ 3 ❍ 4 ❍ 5 ❍ DK ❍	
Tracks progress through performance measurement, audit and feedback, gap analysis, benchmarking, Plan–Do–Study–Acts, change documentation/reporting systems, etc.	1 ❍ 2 ❍ 3 ❍ 4 ❍ 5 ❍ DK ❍	1 ❍ 2 ❍ 3 ❍ 4 ❍ 5 ❍ DK ❍	
Employs mentoring, role modeling, or coaching	1 ❍ 2 ❍ 3 ❍ 4 ❍ 5 ❍ DK ❍	1 ❍ 2 ❍ 3 ❍ 4 ❍ 5 ❍ DK ❍	
Has values congruent with personnel (i.e., shared values, norms, symbols), individual alignment with organization (person-organization fit)	1 ❍ 2 ❍ 3 ❍ 4 ❍ 5 ❍ DK ❍	1 ❍ 2 ❍ 3 ❍ 4 ❍ 5 ❍ DK ❍	
Emphasizes problem solving, error and disagreement resolution, tolerance for risk, surfacing/examining underlying assumptions, mindfulness, and self-awareness	1 ❍ 2 ❍ 3 ❍ 4 ❍ 5 ❍ DK ❍	1 ❍ 2 ❍ 3 ❍ 4 ❍ 5 ❍ DK ❍	
Has a structure/infrastructure that enables change (physical environment, size, spatial dynamics)	1 ❍ 2 ❍ 3 ❍ 4 ❍ 5 ❍ DK ❍	1 ❍ 2 ❍ 3 ❍ 4 ❍ 5 ❍ DK ❍	
Is people-centered (values social interaction, socialization)	1 ❍ 2 ❍ 3 ❍ 4 ❍ 5 ❍ DK ❍	1 ❍ 2 ❍ 3 ❍ 4 ❍ 5 ❍ DK ❍	
Uses shared decisionmaking, collaboration, teamwork, cross-functionality	1 ❍ 2 ❍ 3 ❍ 4 ❍ 5 ❍ DK ❍	1 ❍ 2 ❍ 3 ❍ 4 ❍ 5 ❍ DK ❍	
Allows for autonomy	1 ❍ 2 ❍ 3 ❍ 4 ❍ 5 ❍ DK ❍	1 ❍ 2 ❍ 3 ❍ 4 ❍ 5 ❍ DK ❍	
Selects/retains appropriate personnel	1 ❍ 2 ❍ 3 ❍ 4 ❍ 5 ❍ DK ❍	1 ❍ 2 ❍ 3 ❍ 4 ❍ 5 ❍ DK ❍	
Write-in	1 ❍ 2 ❍ 3 ❍ 4 ❍ 5 ❍ DK ❍	1 ❍ 2 ❍ 3 ❍ 4 ❍ 5 ❍ DK ❍	

APPENDIX E

SME Discussion Summary of Key Drivers of Change for the Army

Driver	Nominations to Top Three	Explanation and Examples
Goals: Sets goals; uses coherent planning, persistence, and strategic/inspirational/innovative thinking; results oriented	Six panelists	This occurs differently at various levels of the organization. In the Army, at the level of senior leadership, this is the description of the general "vision." Subordinate leaders then take this general intent and break it down into specific goals implementable at the relevant level of authority. It is essential that the original vision be clear enough that ambiguities do not result in implementation that contravenes the intent. However, given the variety of different subcultures that exist in an organization as large and diverse as the Army, local autonomy is required to be able to interpret the commander's intent in tandem with the unique local cultural issues.
Accountability: Shared responsibility/accountability	Three panelists	This is part of "leadership." Note that at least one panelist explicitly considered some other drivers (develop personnel/training and role modeling/mentoring/coaching) to be subordinate to this overarching driver of accountability for leaders and managers.[a] One way forward for this driver is to provide training to leaders at all levels on how to both give and receive honest feedback to enable accountability. Bradcasting honest feedup to the recruitment population and to Army personnel could produce greater person-organization fit, as people who are not suited for performance requirements of the Army either do not join or voluntarily leave. Part of accountability is measuring the desired outcome. As noted, it is easier to focus on and measure desired behavioral changes. Appropriate measurement requires an understanding of current culture, and realistic bounds. Note that in many cases the base rate of undesirable behaviors may be low, and goals for changing such a low base rate behavior should take into consideration the effort required to close the behavior gap and weigh that effort against the effort required for closing that gap. Moreover, in some cases some undesired behaviors should be expected to occur and should be seen as learning opportunities. Zero error tolerance is an unforgiving standard which may cause unseen risk, as people game the reporting system rather than focus on true behavior change.

Driver	Nominations to Top Three	Explanation and Examples
Accountability: Shared responsibility/accountability (continued)	Three panelists	Improve execution of existing policy. A great deal of policy and procedure is already on the books, as well as direction on measurements and accountability. Actual improvement at the individual behavioral level and at the aggregate may require a realistic consideration of what behaviors are reinforced, the limitations of resources available (time, personnel energy and cognitive capacity). Determining and setting real priorities among competing imperatives is also part of leadership.
Training: Develops personnel through training, education	Three panelists	This was noted as a vehicle that the military often uses, but one that may not be sufficient to facilitate organizational change. Panelists discussed the importance of targeting training to particular subgroups depending on priorities for each unique group. This is especially necessary given competing demands and limited resources. An example raised was to consider training to a specific problem behavior rather than every possible negative behavior. Training to tiers would suggest that one form of training targets high-level leaders, who can then lead by example to others (enforce and model). Another approach to training is modular training. For example, if women are embedded in a given unit, gender diversity training makes sense; if not, different training may be a higher priority (although members of an all-male unit would have to interact with women in the professional context, and such training would still be important).
Resources: Devoting sufficient resources (financial, staffing, time, etc.) to change efforts	Two panelists	As noted, resources such as time and focus are limited and often conflict with demands. They should be used appropriately and considered in terms of prioritizing culture or climate change. For example, consider the message sent as well as the implications of a given decision taken in the case of a soldier deemed psychologically not ready for combat, when too few soldiers are deployable.
Targeting: Both formal and informal leaders (write-in)	Two panelists	This driver is in some sense included in our ratings (e.g., "stakeholders"). However, the unique component of targeting informal leaders (early adopters, influencers) was considered important enough to highlight separately. Depending on circumstance, informal leaders may include first sergeants, chaplains, and similar people with specific authority, as well as other influencers without any official formally granted authority, job, or rank. Those who volunteer to be change champions may also be included here. Formal leaders are generally readily identifiable in the military hierarchy.
Trust: Focuses on trust, empowerment, self-efficacy, etc.	One panelist	Trust needs to be included in the vision to address the problems of sexual assault and mental health, etc. Leadership should send clear messages that encourage responsible subordinate behavior. For example, a clear message that delaying deployment until an injury resolves is much better than "sucking it up" and risking longer-term challenges. Moreover, subordinates should be able to trust that if they responsibly surface an issue or make a decision within their scope of responsibility, they will not be subject to retaliation. Transparency without fear of reprisal is key. This overlaps with appropriate accountability, discussed above.

Driver	Nominations to Top Three	Explanation and Examples
Mentoring: Role modeling/mentoring/ coaching	One panelist	Role modeling includes which issues leaders think are important and how they react to bad information or negative feedback. Modeled behaviors in this regard will affect how well accountability for desired outcomes actually works. Leadership should send clear messages that encourage responsible subordinate behavior. For example, a clear message could be that delaying deployment until an injury resolves is much better than "sucking it up" and risking longer-term challenges.
Incentives: Applies incentives, encouragement, motivation, or rewards	One panelist	Incentives are not simply the "carrot" or the "stick" but also intrinsic acceptance of a change. As an example, people may agree that reporting sexual abuse is appropriate but it is counter to Army culture because of fear of reprisal. An incentive system must consider intrinsic motivation in addition to monetary and other rewards.
Understand current culture (write-in)	One panelist	As one panelist stated, "If you don't know where you are going, you can't get there."
Selection: Selects/ retains appropriate personnel	One panelist	This driver overlaps with communication and messaging in that people self-select to the message. Therefore, a critical aspect of selecting the desired recruits is to market in a manner that resonates with what they want. Retention and promotion are other opportunities for this mechanism.

[a] Although a leader should be accountable for the appropriate professional development of his or her personnel, this should be considered within realistic bounds. For example, note that some of the issues that may be perceived as endemic to the Army culture may be in fact societal issues, and challenges related to those issues are exacerbated by the relative youth of Army personnel. Young people make mistakes, which can be teachable moments.

Bibliography

Acosta, Joie, Amariah Becker, Jennifer L. Cerully, Michael P. Fisher, Laurie T. Martin, Raffaele Vardavas, Mary Ellen Slaughter, and Terry L. Schell, *Mental Health Stigma in the Military*, Santa Monica, Calif.: RAND Corporation, RR-426-OSD, 2014. As of July 14, 2016: http://www.rand.org/pubs/research_reports/RR426.html

AR—*See* Army Regulation.

Armenakis, Achilles A., Stanley G. Harris, and Hubert S. Feild, "Paradigms in Organizational Change: Change Agent and Change Target Perspectives," in Robert T. Golembiewski, ed., *Handbook of Organizational Behavior*, New York: Marcel Dekker, Inc., 2nd ed., 2001.

Army Regulation 600-100, "Army Leadership," Washington, D.C.: Department of the Army, 2007.

Australian Army, *Army's Future Land Operating Concept*, Canberra: Australian Army Headquarters, 2009.

Bamberger, Peter, "Employee Help-Seeking: Antecedents, Consequences and New Insights for Future Research," *Research in Personnel and Human Resources Management*, Vol. 28, 2009, pp. 49–98.

Bowen, David E., and Cheri Ostroff, "Understanding HRM-Firm Performance Linkages: The Role of the 'Strength' of the HRM System," *Academy of Management Review*, Vol. 29, No. 2, April 2004, pp. 203–221.

Brown, Kenneth G., and Traci Sitzmann, "Training and Employee Development for Improved Performance," in Sheldon Zedeck, ed., *APA Handbook of Industrial and Organizational Psychology*, Vol. 2: *Selecting and Developing Members for the Organization*, Washington, D.C.: American Psychological Association, 2011,
pp. 469–503.

Bucher, Jacob, "General Issue (G.I.) Strain: Applying Strain Theory to Military Offending," *Deviant Behavior*, Vol. 32, No. 9, 2011, pp. 846–875.

Burke, Lisa A., and Holly M. Hutchins, "Training Transfer: An Integrative Literature Review," *Human Resource Development Review*, Vol. 6, No. 3, 2007, pp. 263–296.

Burke, Wyatt Warner, *Organizational Change: Theory and Practice*, Thousand Oaks, Calif.: Sage, 2002.

———, "A Perspective on the Field of Organization Development and Change: The Zeigarnik Effect," *Journal of Applied Behavioral Science*, Vol. 47, No. 2, 2011, pp. 143–167.

———, "Organizational Change," in Benjamin Schneider and Karen M. Barbera, eds., *The Oxford Handbook of Organizational Climate and Culture*, New York: Oxford University Press, 1st ed., 2014.

Campbell, Constance, "A Longitudinal Study of One Organization's Culture: Do Values Endure?" *American Journal of Business*, Vol. 19, No. 2, 2004. pp. 41–52.

Church, Allan H., Alan G. Walker, and Joel Brockner, "Multisource Feedback for Organizational Development and Change," in Janine Waclawski and Allan H. Church, eds., *Organizational Development: Data Driven Methods for Change*, San Francisco: Jossey-Bass, 2002, pp. 27–54.

Cottingham, Ann H., Anthony L. Suchman, Debra K. Litzelman, Richard M. Frankel, David L. Mossbarger, Penelope R. Williamson, DeWitt C. Bargain, and Thomas S. Inui, "Enhancing the Informal Curriculum of a Medical School: A Case Study in Organizational Culture Change," *Journal of General Internal Medicine*, Vol. 23, 2008, pp. 715–722.

Dalal, Reeshad S., "A Meta-Analysis of the Relationship Between Organizational Citizenship Behavior and Counterproductive Work Behavior," *Journal of Applied Psychology*, Vol. 90, No. 6, 2005, pp. 1241–1255.

Day, David V., Mark A. Griffin, and Kim R. Louw, "The Climate and Culture of Leadership in Organizations," Benjamin Schneider and Karen M. Barbera, eds., *The Oxford Handbook of Organizational Climate and Culture*, New York: Oxford University Press, 2014, pp. 101–117.

Denison, Daniel R., "What Is the Difference Between Organizational Culture and Organizational Climate? A Native's Point of View on a Decade of Paradigm Wars," *The Academy of Management Review*, Vol. 21, No. 3, 1996, pp. 619–654.

Ehrhart, Mark G., Benjamin Schneider, and William H. Macey, *Organizational Climate and Culture: An Introduction to Theory, Research, and Practice*, New York: Routledge, 2014.

Farris, Coreen, and Kimberley A. Hepner, *Targeting Alcohol Misuse: A Promising Strategy for Reducing Military Sexual Assaults?* Santa Monica, Calif.: RAND Corporation, RR-538-OSD, 2014. As of July 14, 2016:
http://www.rand.org/pubs/research_reports/RR538.html

Fernandez, Sergio, and Hal G. Rainey, "Managing Successful Organizational Change in the Public Sector," *Public Administration Review*, Vol. 66, No. 2, 2006, pp. 168–176.

Ford, J. Kevin, and Pennie Foster-Fishman, "Organizational Development and Change: Linking Research from the Profit, Nonprofit, and Public Sectors," in Steve. J. Kozlowski, ed., *The Oxford Handbook of Organizational Psychology*, New York: Oxford University Press, Vol. 2, 2012, pp. 956–992.

Glisson, Charles, Anthony Hemmelgarn, Philip Green, Denzel Dukes, Shannon Atkinson, and Nathaniel J. Williams, "Randomized Trial of the Availability, Responsiveness, and Continuity (ARC) Organizational Intervention with Community-Based Mental Health Programs and Clinicians Serving Youth," *Journal of the American Academy of Child & Adolescent Psychiatry*, Vol. 51, No. 8, August 2012, pp. 780–787.

González-Romá, Vicente, and Ana Hernández, "Climate Uniformity: Its Influence on Team Communication Quality, Task Conflict, and Team Performance," *Journal of Applied Psychology*, Vol. 99, No. 6, 2014, pp. 1042–1058.

Great Britain Health and Safety Commission, *ASCNI Human Factors Study Group: Organizing for Safety, Third Report*, London: H.M. Stationery Office, 1993.

Gruys, Melissa L., and Paul R. Sackett, "Investigating the Dimensionality of Counterproductive Work Behavior," *International Journal of Selection and Assessment*, Vol. 11, No. 1, 2003, pp. 30–42.

Hauck, Sheila, Rebecca P. Winsett, and Judy Kuric, "Leadership Facilitation Strategies to Establish Evidence-Based Practice in an Acute Care Hospital," *Journal of Advanced Nursing*, Vol. 69, No. 3, 2013, pp. 664–674.

Hofstede, Geert, and Gert Jan Hofstede, *Cultures and Organization: Software of the Mind*, 2nd ed., New York: McGraw -Hill, 2005.

Kotter, John P., "Leading Change: Why Transformation Efforts Fail," *Harvard Business Review*, 1995, pp. 59–67.

Lewin, Kurt, "Frontiers in Group Dynamics: Concept, Method and Reality in Social Science; Social Equilibria and Social Change," *Human Relations*, Vol. 1, No. 1, 1947, pp. 5–41.

Martin, Joanne, and Caren Siehl, "Organizational Culture and Counterculture: An Uneasy Symbiosis," *Organizational Dynamics*, Vol. 12, No. 2, 1983, pp. 52–64.

Martins, Luis L., "Organizational Change and Development," in Sheldon Zedeck, ed., *APA Handbook of Industrial and Organizational Psychology*, Washington, D.C.: American Psychological Association, 1st ed.,
Vol. 3, 2011.

Meaney, Mark E., "Error Reduction, Patient Safety and Institutional Ethics Committees," *The Journal of Law, Medicine & Ethics*, Vol. 32, No. 2, 2004, pp. 358–364.

Meredith, Lisa S., Cathy D. Sherbourne, Sarah Gaillot, Lydia Hansell, Hans V. Ritschard, Andrew M. Parker, and Glenda Wrenn, *Promoting Psychological Resilience in the U.S. Military*, Santa Monica, Calif.: RAND Corporation, MG-996-OSD, 2011. As of July 14, 2016:
http://www.rand.org/pubs/monographs/MG996.html

Military Leadership Diversity Commission, *From Representation to Inclusion: Diversity Leadership for the 21st-Century Military*, Arlington, Va.: Military Leadership Diversity Commission, 2011.

Miller, Laura L., Jennifer Kavanagh, Maria C. Lytell, Keith Jennings, and Craig Martin, *The Extent of Restrictions on the Service of Active-Component Military Women*, Santa Monica, Calif.: RAND Corporation, MG-1175-OSD, 2012. As of July 14, 2016:
http://www.rand.org/pubs/monographs/MG1175.html

Morral, Andrew R., Kristie L. Gore, and Terry L. Schell, *Sexual Assault and Sexual Harassment in the U.S. Military:* Volume 1. *Design of the 2014 RAND Military Workplace Study*, Santa Monica, Calif.: RAND Corporation, RR-870/1-OSD, 2014. As of July 14, 2016:
http://www.rand.org/pubs/research_reports/RR870z1.html

Munroe, Donna J., Poonam L. Kaza, and David Howard, "Culture-Change Training: Nursing Facility Staff Perceptions of Culture Change," *Geriatric Nursing*, Vol. 32, No. 6, 2011, pp. 400–407.

National Defense Research Institute, *Sexual Orientation and U.S. Military Personnel Policy: An Update of RAND's 1993 Study*, Santa Monica, Calif: RAND Corporation, MG-1056-OSD, 2010. As of July 14, 2016:
http://www.rand.org/pubs/monographs/MG1056.html

Newman, Daniel A., Ted Kinney, and James L. Farr, "Job Performance Ratings," in *Comprehensive Handbook of Psychological Assessment*, Jay Thomas, ed., Vol. 4, 2003, pp. 373–389.

Ostroff, Cheri, Angelo J. Kinicki, and Rabiah Muhammad, "Organizational Culture and Climate," in Irving B. Weiner, Neal W. Schmitt, and Scott Highhouse, eds., *Handbook of Psychology*, Hoboken, N.J.: John Wiley & Sons, Vol. 12, 2012, pp. 643–676.

Ostroff, Cheri, Angelo J. Kinicki, and Melinda M. Tamkins, "Organizational Culture and Climate," in Walter C. Borman, Daniel R. Ilgen, and Richard J. Klimoski, eds., *Handbook of Psychology: Industrial and Organizational Psychology*, Hoboken, N.J.: John Wiley & Sons, Vol. 12, 2003, pp. 565–593.

Ramchand, Rajeev, Joie Acosta, Rachel M. Burns, Lisa H. Jaycox, and Christopher G. Pernin, *The War Within: Preventing Suicide in the U.S. Military*, Santa Monica, Calif.: RAND Corporation, MG-953-OSD, 2011. As of July 14, 2016:
http://www.rand.org/pubs/monographs/MG953.html

Robinson, Sandra L., and Rebecca J. Bennett, "A Typology of Deviant Workplace Behaviors: A Multidimensional Scaling Study," *Academy of Management Journal*, Vol. 38, No. 2, 1995, pp. 555–572.

Schein, Edgar H., *Organizational Psychology*, Englewood Cliffs, N.J.: Prentice Hall, 1965.

———, *Organizational Culture and Leadership: A Dynamic View*, 1st ed., San Francisco: Jossey-Bass, 1985.

——— "Organizational Culture," *American Psychologist*, Vol. 45, No. 2, 1990, pp. 109–119.

———, *Organizational Culture and Leadership*, 2nd ed., San Francisco: Jossey-Bass, 1992.

———, *Organizational Culture and Leadership*, 3rd ed., San Francisco: Jossey-Bass, John Wiley & Sons, 2004.

———, *Organizational Culture and Leadership*, 4th ed., San Francisco: Jossey-Bass, 2010.

Schlager, Melinda D., "An Assessment of Parole Officer and Administrator Attitudes on Organizational Culture and Parole Supervision in a Northeastern State," *Journal of Offender Rehabilitation*, Vol. 47, No. 3, 2008, pp. 271–289.

Schneider, Benjamin, Mark G. Ehrhart, and William H. Macey, "Perspectives on Organizational Climate and Culture," in Sheldon Zedeck, ed., *APA Handbook of Industrial and Organizational Psychology*, Washington, D.C.: American Psychological Association, 2011, pp. 373–414.

Schneider, Benjamin, Harold W. Goldstein, and D. Brent Smith, "The ASA Framework: An Update," *Personnel Psychology*, Vol. 48, 1995, pp. 747–773.

Schroeder, Peter J., and Jay P. Scribner, " 'To Honor and Glorify God': The Role of Religion in One Intercollegiate Athletics Culture," *Sport Education and Society*, Vol. 11, No. 1, 2006, pp. 39–54.

Simpson, D. Dwayne, George W. Joe, and Grace A. Rowan-Szal, "Linking the Elements of Change: Program and Client Responses to Innovation," *Journal of Substance Abuse Treatment*, Vol. 33, No. 2, 2007, pp. 201–209.

Soeters, Joseph L., "Culture in Uniformed Organizations," in Neal. M. Ashkanasy, Celeste P. M. Wilderom, and Mark F. Peterson, eds., *Handbook of Organizational Culture and Climate*, Thousand Oaks, Calif.: Sage Publications, 2000.

United States Army Combined Arms Center, *The Human Dimension White Paper: A Framework for Optimizing Human Performance*, October 9, 2014.

United States Army Medical Department, "Ready and Resilient Campaign (R2C)," web page, undated. As of July 14, 2016:
http://phc.amedd.army.mil/topics/healthyliving/hpr/Pages/ReadyandResilientCampaign.aspx

United States Department of Defense, *2011 Department of Defense Health Related Behaviors Survey of Active Duty Military Personnel*, Fairfax, Va.: ICF International, 2013.

Walker, Nefertiti A., and Melanie L. Sartore-Baldwin, "Hegemonic Masculinity and the Institutionalized Bias Toward Women in Men's Collegiate Basketball: What Do Men Think?" *Journal of Sport Management*, Vol. 27, 2013, pp. 303–315.

Wong, Leonard, Paul Bliese, and Dennis McGurk, "Military Leadership: A Context Specific Review," *Leadership Quarterly*, Vol. 14, No. 6, 2003, pp. 657–692.

Zohar, Dov, and David Hofmann, "Organizational Culture and Climate," in Steve J. Kozlowski, eds., *The Oxford Handbook of Organizational Psychology*, New York: Oxford University Press, Vol. 1, 2012, pp. 643–666.

Zohar, Dov, and Tal Polachek, "Discourse-Based Intervention for Modifying Supervisory Communication as Leverage for Safety Climate and Performance Improvement: A Randomized Field Study," Journal of Applied Psychology, Vol. 99, No. 1, January 2014, pp. 113–124.